# TASTING
## Club

# TASTING *Club*

## GATHERING TOGETHER TO SHARE
## AND SAVOR YOUR FAVORITE TASTES

Written by Dina Cheney
Photographed by Charles Schiller

London, New York, Munich, Melbourne, and Delhi

Senior Editor   Anja Schmidt
Designer   Jee Chang
Managing Art Editor   Michelle Baxter
Art Director   Dirk Kaufman
DTP Coordinator   Kathy Farias
Production Manager   Ivor Parker
Executive Managing Editor   Sharon Lucas
Publisher   Carl Raymond

Prop Stylist   Bette Blau
Prop assistant   Kristine Trevino
Food Stylists   Tracey Harlor and Patricia White
All photography by Charles Schiller, unless noted below:
Page 54: Jupiter Images; Page 144: DK Images
Photographer's Assistant   Armando Rafaei

Published by DK Publishing, Inc., 375 Hudson Street, New York,
New York 10014

06 07 08 09 10 9 8 7 6 5 4 3 2 1

A catalog record for this book is available from the Library of
Congress.

ISBN 0-7566-2059-7
Color reproduction by Colourscan, Singapore
Printed and bound in China by Leo Paper Products Ltd

Discover more at www.dk.com

# •CONTENTS•

# THE BASICS

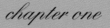

*chapter one*

Breaking bread with others in your own home is one of life's best experiences. The problem is, few of us have the time or the know-how to actually bake the bread (and roast the chicken, and toss the salad, and so forth). Meanwhile, those of us who can and do cook complicated meals often find ourselves looking for something novel.

At-home tastings are a new, fun, low-hassle way to entertain. For these delicious, educational events, the host gathers variations on one type of food or beverage. Then, everyone *deep-tastes*, or slowly savors the food and drink in a structured fashion, to get super-acquainted with their palates. During the tasting, guests record their observations, learn, laugh, and enjoy. Even better: no cooking is necessary, and clean-up is minimal!

## How do I taste?

Although many of us give full credit to our taste buds, most of what we call our sense of taste, in fact, comes from our sense of smell. That's because taste buds—located on the tongue, the insides of the cheeks, the roof of the mouth, and in the throat—can only detect four basic tastes: sweet, salty, sour, and bitter. Some scientists have also identified a fifth taste, called umami (savory), characteristic of MSG, seaweed, and wild mushrooms. (Some believe that certain regions of the tongue can detect certain tastes most, as per the map of the tongue below.) Since our taste buds are located throughout our mouths, it's important to spread food and drink all around them when deep-tasting.

Our nasal passages, on the other hand, can detect thousands of distinct smells or aromas, carried through the air by molecules in foods and drinks. Because our sense of smell is so fundamental to our perception of food and drink items, it's critical not to overwhelm it with strong odors (such as perfume, cologne, incense, or aromatic flowers or plants) and not to have a cold when deep-tasting.

## When should tastings be held?

Tastings, which last anywhere from 1½ to 3 hours, can take place any time of day, any day of the week. However, unless you're arranging a work-related event, I recommend weekends, when your guests will be relaxed and can enjoy the tasting experience.

Whereas some types of tastings (such as chocolate, beer, and wine) are best for evenings, others (such as tea and honey) are perfect for the morning or afternoon. When determining the time of each event, just think about what you're offering and what time of day you'd prefer to try it.

It also makes sense to hold certain tastings at particular times of the year. For example, since the largest variety of apples is available in the fall, host your apple tasting then. During hot summers, refresh your guests with a beer tasting, and in the harsh winter, invite people over for rich, satisfying chocolate (perhaps around Valentine's Day). Consider celebrating the seasons with a white wine tasting in June and a red wine tasting in December. Finally, while a wide array of fresh vegetables is in season, a balsamic vinegar or extra virgin olive oil tasting might be in order (just imagine serving the condiments with ripe heirloom tomatoes and sea salt).

## Where should i hold a tasting?

Tastings can be held anywhere, from your home, to a park, to a conference room. However, I recommend staying indoors—that way, you won't have to contend with the weather (a hot day and melting chocolate!) or particularly gregarious bees.

Situate the event around a large, wide table, perhaps in your dining room or kitchen. You want everyone comfortably seated so that they can concentrate on the tasting. Soft music, such as classical or New Age, can contribute to the atmosphere, but make sure it's not too distracting.

## How does a tasting club work, exactly?

If you decide to form a tasting club, take turns hosting these events with your friends. Whoever is hosting can be responsible for providing everything. This is the simplest strategy; however, the cost of tastings can vary dramatically with the price of the food and drink. For example, balsamic vinegar, wine, and extra virgin olive oil tastings are more expensive than apple and chocolate tastings. To resolve this, your tasting club might decide to have everyone bring cash or a check to each event to reimburse the host. The amount can vary depending on the cost of each tasting, or your group can decide on a fixed amount, such as $30-$50 per person or couple (leftover money can be used for a treat for everyone).

Alternatively, each guest or couple can bring one sample to each event; if you go this route, the host needs to give everyone the lowdown on how to purchase the items (each chapter offers this information) and either tell them what to buy or find out what they plan to purchase in advance. (No one wants three hunks of Parmigiano-Reggiano!) The only drawback here is that the samples can't be organized and set out prior to the event (although this is only an issue for tea and chocolate). The host should just know that, for those events, he or she will need about 15 minutes after the guests arrive to set up.

As a final option, your club might decide to have each guest or couple bring a bottle of wine or a few bottles of beer to each tasting. Where alcohol is less appropriate (as with tea, honey, and apples), attendees could bring accompaniments, such as fresh fruit, nuts, cheese, tea sandwiches, or other hors d'oeuvres. Again, the host should either tell everyone what to bring or ask each guest what they plan to buy in advance.

## How should i conduct a tasting?

Determine what type of tasting you'll be hosting and plan the menu. Begin by considering yourself and your (potential) guests and deciding how much (or how little) you want to spend. Ask yourself what types of food and drinks everyone likes and how knowledgeable they are about them. For novices, host an introductory tasting, where you include different varieties of the food or drink item. For experts, consider narrowing the range to a specific type. For example, in the case of a tea tasting, you could serve blacks, oolongs, and greens for novices, or all greens for experts.

After you decide on the tasting category, determine which food or drink items will accompany the samples. Although professional tasters cleanse their palates with unsalted crackers, neutral-flavored bread, and water, you'll want to make your tasting more fun (and palatable). So, have fun with the accompaniments. Each chapter of this book includes helpful hints on pairing.

Keep in mind that you can serve store-bought accompaniments, prepare a few things yourself, or ask your guests to bring drinks or dishes (such as hors d'oeuvres for a wine tasting or even wine for a cured meats tasting). Since alcohol adds conviviality, it's a good idea to figure out how to include it.

INVITE YOUR GUESTS. Your goal should be 6 to 12 people (including you) at each tasting (I think 8 is the ideal size). Remember that you'll need to fit them around a table, and you'll want to give everyone a chance to share their observations. (For a tea tasting, where you'll need to boil water and steep tea during the event, stick with a smaller group, ideally 6 to 8.) Make sure to include the following on the invitation:

- The type of food/drink item to be tasted (such as dark chocolate), as well as the full menu (That way, your guests will know whether they should eat beforehand and, if they don't like the featured type of food or drink, they can skip the event.)
- A request not to wear perfume or cologne (which would interfere with everyone's olfactory abilities)
- A request to RSVP by a certain date

You might want to ask a guest to serve as your helper during the event (especially important at tea tastings). Once you've received your guests' RSVPs, purchase the necessary materials. Just consult the list of "The Basics" on the next page, as well as the supplementary lists of items provided in each chapter. Keep in mind that disposable cups, plates, bowls, flatware, and, of course, napkins, can be used. Although they might detract from the mood, they simplify clean-up and cut the expense.

## The Basics

- ⁊ This book, opened to the appropriate chapter.

- ⁊ Pens—1 for everyone, including you.

- ⁊ To make the tasting grids easier to use, xerox them to 150–200% in size. The guests and hosts can record their impressions of the food and drink items on this grid, which is different for each chapter. If you'd prefer a less formal note-taking format, dispense with the grids altogether and give everyone a clean sheet of paper. Either way, have guests take them home.)

- ⁊ Copies of the menu—1 for everyone, including you. (The menu should list the samples and other foods and drinks being served—see the chapters for examples. Guests should take these home.)

- ⁊ Drinks and food, including hors d'oeuvres (if serving), samples, accompaniments, and desserts (if serving). (Figure on six samples per tasting.)

- ⁊ Napkins, plates (try simple white to set off the colors of the food), utensils, and wine or beer glasses, if appropriate.

- ⁊ Glasses or cups filled with cold (but not ice-cold) water (for cleansing the palate and keeping guests hydrated).

The following materials are useful and worth purchasing if you plan to host a few tastings: platters; serving bowls; a plate stand (for a multi-tiered presentation—of fruit, tea sandwiches, scones, cookies, and more); a pitcher (for water); an attractive bucket (for discarding drinks, used spoons, etc.); and index cards and labels (for identifying samples).

PREPARE FOR THE TASTING by shopping, cooking (if necessary), setting the table, and organizing the samples. Each chapter guides you through these processes. Keep in mind, though, that for most tastings, you'll want to smell and taste the products in advance, arranging them in order from mildest to strongest for tasting.

CONDUCT THE TASTING. Each tasting is structured in the following way (keep in mind that this format is optional—feel free to tailor it to your group's preferences): When guests arrive, serve them a "welcome" drink and some food, or just get right into the tasting. Once everyone's seated, take turns reading aloud some introductory information and trivia from the chapter about the food or drink item. (This step is optional, but recommended, since it gets everyone involved right away and gives them context for the tasting.) Pass around the first sample and guide the group through tasting it in a structured fashion. Meanwhile, have everyone record their thoughts in their "Tasting Grid."

Once they've written their thoughts, discuss the sample as a group. Then have everyone cleanse their palates (with water and bread or crackers) to prepare for the next sample. The tasting portions from this point on should be self-guided, but you can certainly discuss the remaining items as you go. Feel free to take conversation breaks throughout.

After all the samples have been tasted, discuss what you thought about them and partake in additional food and drink. Encourage your guests to take home their menus and grids.

## LET THE TASTINGS BEGIN!

Professional tasters are purists. They remove all distractions—that means no Port with their chocolate when working! In most cases, they also taste blindly, meaning without knowledge of brand or product names. Since we're not professionals, we can have a little more fun. So, encourage conversation and laughter and don't take your tastings too seriously.

## Recommended Events

- Chocolate tasting for a bridal shower, a bachelorette party, a company team-building session, or after a romantic Valentine's Day dinner.
- Tea tasting for a knitting party, book discussion, women's spa day, or baby shower.
- Beer tasting for a Super Bowl™ party or weekly poker game.
- Balsamic vinegar or extra virgin olive oil tasting for a garden tour (where the condiments are served with bounty from the garden) or Italian conversation club meeting.
- (French) cheese tasting for a French conversation club meeting.
- Honey tasting for an afternoon tea, or honey and apple tastings for Rosh Hashanah.
- Hanukkah party with apple picking, an apple tasting, and applesauce- and latke-making.
- Christmas buffet with an antipasto platter and a cured meats tasting.
- New Year's Eve cocktail party with a cheese and/or wine tasting.
- Small family reunion with any of the tastings.

# "BLIND" VERSUS "NON-BLIND" TASTING

You'll find that the tastings in this book are not blind, meaning that guests know the identity of each product before sampling it. I have hosted both blind and non-blind tastings and have found that the added effort of disguising the samples is usually not worth it—especially since most people aren't connoisseurs of extra virgin olive oil or honey anyway. Also, by the time you reveal information about the products, your guests may have forgotten what they tasted like. Thus, I recommend sticking with non-blind tastings. They're just as interesting and educational as blind tastings (if not more so), and easier to host. One notable exception: wine and beer tastings. These can be worth hosting blind, especially if you feature highly-famed, expensive bottles alongside inexpensive ones. In those cases, just place the bottles in numbered brown paper bags.

# WINE

*chapter two*

Cherries, leather, tobacco, black pepper—a single glass of wine can encapsulate an entire world of flavors. Just swirl, sniff, sip, and submit to pure, unadulterated seduction. Yet, wine is more than merely sensual: this age-old beverage expresses the land from which it hails and the grapes from which it is made.

With literally thousands of grape varieties and wine-producing areas, though, you may be wondering where to begin. Luckily, learning about wine need not be overwhelming or intimidating. Although somewhat complicated, this most rewarding subject is particularly well-suited to tastings. So, gather together a few bottles and friends and begin your education. Cheers!

# KNOW YOUR WINE

Although wine—in essence, fermented grape juice—is most often associated with Europe (and France in particular), high-quality *vino* is actually produced all over the world, including Italy, Spain, Germany, the United States, Australia, New Zealand, Chile, South Africa, and Argentina.

It all starts with the grape-growing process, or *viticulture*. While there are thousands of grape varieties, several—Chardonnay, Sauvignon Blanc, Riesling, Pinot Noir, Shiraz/Syrah (they're the same thing), Cabernet Sauvignon, and Merlot—make up the majority grown and used in wine.

Some wines, such as Chablis (a French white wine), are made with one grape variety, while others, such as Bordeaux, consist of blends. Along with adding complexity, blending helps to balance out the occasionally too-strong traits of certain types of grapes.

The characteristics of wine result, in large part, from the properties of the grapes from which they're made. For example, the Gewürztraminer grape produces spicy, highly aromatic white wines, while the Gamay grape yields light-bodied, red wines, such as Beaujolais. (See the "Grape Varieties" chart on page 27.)

## The Importance of Terroir

There's more to wine than just grape variety, though: where and how the grapes are grown are critical too. The French use the term *terroir* to describe the agricultural area's soil, elevation, and climate. Certain places are thought to produce superior grapes, and thus carry a good amount of prestige; in many cases, these premium areas can be as small as individual villages or even vineyards. In fact, it's usually the case that the more specific the growing area designated on the label, the higher-quality the wine.

The designation of these top-of-the-line areas is not random: often, they feature dry soil and, sometimes, they're at high elevations. These qualities force the grapes to struggle, resulting in more complex and flavorful fruit and juice. (Older vines and lower vineyard yields—the latter achieved largely through vigorous pruning—also result in more flavorful grapes.)

*Wine can also be made with other types of fruit, such as plums or blackberries.*

Additionally, some areas are particularly well-suited to certain grape varieties. For example, many white (actually, yellow or green) grapes have the ability to grow in harsher or cooler climates, such as Alsace, France. On the other hand, red (actually, blue, purple, or red) grapes tend to be more sensitive to climate and are usually grown in warmer areas, such as Southern Italy. Accordingly, then, France's warm Northern Rhône Valley is known for its wines made from (red) Syrah grapes, while cooler Germany is associated with wines made from (white) Rieslings.

Climate is so important that, to a certain extent, it can dictate the flavor of the grape. Grapes tend not to ripen as much in cooler climates. As a result, they have more acidity, and less body (concentration), fruitiness, and tannin (a mouth-drying quality, as with overly steeped black tea, walnuts, or unripe persimmons). Warmer climates, on the other hand, can grow much riper grapes, resulting in lower acidity and greater body, fruitiness, and tannins.

As wine expert Andrea Immer Robinson spells out in *Great Wine Made Simple,* certain fruit flavors are associated with specific climates: Cooler climates produce white grapes with apple, pear, and quince flavors and red grapes with cherry, cranberry, red currant, and pomegranate flavors. Moderate climates yield white grapes with citrus, stone fruit, melon, and kiwifruit flavors and red grapes with blueberry, strawberry, raspberry, blackberry, black currant, and plum notes. Warm climates, on the other hand, grow white grapes with tropical fruit flavors and red grapes that are reminiscent of figs, raisins, and prunes.

Along with the vineyard's distance from the equator, weather has a marked impact on grapes and wine. Both wet and dry weather are essential for a great harvest—rain in the earlier part of the season helps the vines grow, while a long period of dry weather before harvesting keeps the grapes from becoming watery and moldy. Severe weather, such as heavy rainstorms, can result in grapes with bland, diluted juice. It's these climatic fluctuations that determine which years, called "vintages," are considered good and bad. In areas with more climatic variation—especially in Europe—vintages are even more important.

More than 10,000 varieties of wine grapes exist. Most of them are members of the species *Vitis vinifera*. Others, including Seyval Blanc and Baco Noir, are hybrids of the two.

## How Wine is Made

The wine-making process, called *vinification*, varies depending on the type and style of wine being produced. While white wine, such as Sauvignon Blanc, is usually made with white grapes, red wine, such as Shiraz, is produced from red grapes. Rosé is made with red grapes (though white grapes can be added).

Typically, wine production begins with the pressing or crushing of the grapes. For white wines, the resulting mixture is filtered and then transferred into oak barrels or stainless steel vats, where *fermentation* (the conversion of the sugars in the juice to alcohol, by yeasts) takes place. For red and rosé wines, the mixture is not initially filtered. Instead, the juice is fermented along with the skins and sometimes seeds, a process known as *maceration*. Since the skins and seeds (and stems) contain pigments and tannins (those mouth-drying substances), it is from maceration that red wines attain their color and texture.

The longer the maceration period, the more pigments and tannins transfer to the juice. For this reason, winemakers stop the process quickly for rosé and some very light red wines. If winemakers want their product to feature a lot of residual (leftover) sugar, they'll halt the fermentation process early as well, before the yeasts convert all the sugars to alcohol. They do this either by dropping the temperature or by adding more alcohol to the juice or wine. (At a concentration of 15% alcohol, the yeasts die.)

After fermentation, the wine is aged, either in stainless steel or oak barrels. Whether oak is used—for aging and fermentation—is extremely important (most experts believe that oak has more of an impact with aging). Oak barrels imbue wines with smoky, toasty, vanilla-y, and spicy flavors, as well as tannins, and a fuller body. Newer, smaller barrels that have been heated more during their production add more character than older, larger barrels that have been heated or charred less.

Since oak barrels are very expensive, most wineries use them only for their best grapes, and, naturally, charge a premium for doing so. Winemakers who want to add oakiness to their products without the expense sometimes use oak strips, chips, or even flavorings.

## THE STORY OF CHAMPAGNE

True Champagne, produced using the *méthode Champenoise*, is made from Pinot Noir (red), Pinot Meunier (red), and Chardonnay (white) grapes. After the grapes are harvested and pressed, their juice is fermented (sometimes in oak for a fuller body), then

# DIFFERENT TYPES OF WINE

The discussion in these pages has primarily concerned table wines, which include white, red, and rosé. These wines are still (not sparkling), feature from 7–15% alcohol, and are generally dry (not sweet). There are, however, several other types of wine, including sparkling, dessert, and fortified.

Sparkling wines, including (French) Champagne and (Italian) Prosecco and Asti Spumante, contain less alcohol than table wines, and undergo a secondary fermentation, whereby carbonation (bubbles) is generated. While many of these wines are inexpensive, Champagne (with a capital "C") can only be produced in the Champagne region of France, and is sometimes very pricey. Most of the less expensive sparklers (with the exception of the Spanish Cava) undergo secondary fermentation in a large tank, while the more costly versions are fermented for the second time in the bottle and held for years before being sold.

Dessert wine results from grapes that have been dried (Italian vin santo),
frozen (ice wine or *eiswein*), infected with botrytis mold, known as "noble rot" (French Sauternes), or harvested extremely late in the season (late harvest Rieslings; Hungarian Tokaji; French Vouvray Moelleux; and German Auslese, Beerenauslese, and Trockenbeerenauslese). In all cases, the grapes become extremely concentrated in flavor, resulting in super-sweet, and often, more alcoholic wines.

Since producing dessert wine is time-consuming and risky—as bad weather or birds might destroy the grapes before they're harvested—it's often very expensive.

Finally, fortified wines, including Port or Porto (from Northern Portugal), Sherry (from Southern Spain), Madeira, Marsala, and Vermouth, can be dry or sweet and are "fortified" by the addition of alcohol. Vin Doux Naturel is a category of fortified French dessert wines (including Muscat Beaumes-de-Venise and Banyuls), where the grapes are dried, and alcohol is added during the fermentation process.

blended. At this point, *liqueur de triage* (a mixture of sugar and yeast) is added, and a secondary fermentation takes place—this time, in the permanent bottle (but with a temporary bottle cap). Bubbles (from carbon dioxide) as well as sediment result from this process. After aging, the bottles are riddled (placed neck-down on racks and turned for weeks). In a step known as *dégorgement*, the tops of the bottles are then frozen (with brine), and the caps and frozen sediments are removed. Next, in dosage, wine and sugar are added—the proportion determines the sweetness of the resulting Champagne. Finally, the bottles are recorked.

## Old World Versus New World

The wine world often differentiates between "Old World" and "New World" wines, the former referring to those produced in Europe and the latter to those produced outside of Europe, including in the United States, Australia, and New Zealand. It's that simple. While Old World wines, such as Puligny-Montrachet, are usually named for where they're made (in this case, a French village), New World wines, such as Pinot Noir from Oregon (USA) or Australian Shiraz, are usually named for the grapes from which they're made. Because grape variety determines these wines' names, they're known as *varietals*.

> The average bottle of wine contains 750 milliliters or about 25 fluid ounces (5 glasses).

Appropriately, while Old World wines are usually more restrained and earthy in flavor and express their *terroir*, New World wines tend to express the grapes from which they're produced, resulting in bolder and fruitier (or more "fruit-forward") flavors.

Because of their longer wine-making histories, many European nations legislate exactly how certain types of wine should be made—specifically, which grape varieties should be used, exactly where they should be grown, and how the wine should be produced, down to alcohol levels and minimum aging periods. For example, a Chablis cannot be labeled as such unless it is made with 100% Chardonnay grapes from the Chablis region of France. The French AOC; Italian DOC or DOCG; and Spanish DO, which you will see on wine labels, refer to these different regulations.

On the other hand, New World winemakers are generally free to experiment with different grape blends, wine-growing areas, and technologies, as they're not under the stricture of as many laws.

Recently, some Old World winemakers have been producing wines with proprietary—or, basically, made-up—names, such as the Tuscan "Ornellaia." By doing so, they have the liberty of making high-quality wines that do not fall under the aegis of the DOC and other laws regarding grape varieties, growing areas, and prestige designations.

# WHEN WINE AGES

Generally, premium (i.e. expensive) wines, including prestige Bordeaux, Vintage Ports, and Barolos and Barbarescos, are most suited to the aging process.

When wine ages, it becomes less acidic and fruity, and its tannins soften or attenuate. Perhaps most attractive to wine connoisseurs, it also develops all sorts of interesting new aromas and flavors.

Aging even changes the color of wine. While red wine becomes lighter, white wine actually darkens.

Finally, many prestigious Old World wines (such as Italian Barolo and Barbaresco) feature high levels of tannin and are meant to age for years. New World wines, on the other hand, tend to feature lower tannin levels and are often meant for more immediate consumption (tannins, along with acid and alcohol, help to preserve wine).

## Wine Laws

Different countries have different laws for what percentage of a particular type of wine needs to be made from a particular variety of grape to be called by that grape's name; for example 85% in Germany, 80% in Australia, 75% in the United States (100%

in Oregon, with the exception of 90% minimum for Cabernet Sauvignon), and 100% in Alsace, France.

Similarly, different countries have different laws for what percentage of a wine needs to come from grapes grown in a particular area to be marketed as hailing from that area; for example 85% in the United States and Australia.

In terms of alcohol content, in the United States, the actual percentage of alcohol can be 1.5% higher or lower than the amount stated on the label; however, it cannot go over 14% without explicitly stating so.

Finally, when it comes to vintages, different countries have different laws for what percentage of a wine needs to come from a specific harvest to be labeled with that year; for example 85% for Germany, and 95% for both Australia and the United States.

## GRAPE VARIETIES

About 50 types of white grapes and 40 types of red grapes are grown on a large scale worldwide. By learning the characteristics of the different grapes, you'll be better able to predict the nature of different bottles of wine. Use the chart on the opposite page by itself for New World wines (called *varietals*), and in conjunction with the table on page 29 for Old World wines. Remember to consider these two tables alongside factors such as climate and general New World versus Old World wine characteristics. Also important to consider are tannins and acid: while the former are a key factor in red wines, the latter is central with whites.

## *Classified* GRAPE ☞ KEY ☜

✳ **RED GRAPES**
Other popular red grapes include Dolcetto (fruity and low-acid, from Piedmont), Barbera (acidic, also from Piedmont), Cabernet Franc (from Bordeaux), Grenache or Garnacha (fruity—the first is the French name and the second is the Spanish name), Malbec (now prevalent in Argentina), Petit Verdot (from Bordeaux), Nero d'Avola (from Sicily), Primitivo (from Southern Italy), Carmenere (from Bordeaux and Chile), Petit Sirah (grown in California), Mourvedre (popular in Spain and Southern France), and Pinotage (grown in South Africa).

▨ **WHITE GRAPES**
Other popular white grapes include Pinot Blanc (grown in Alsace and California), Vernaccia di San Gimignano (from Tuscany), and Arneis (from Italy's Piedmont region).

| ·NAME· | ·CHARACTERISTICS· | ·TYPE· | ·REGION· |
|---|---|---|---|
| ❊ Gamay | Very light-bodied, very low tannins, fresh, fruity, acidic | Beaujolais | Beaujolais (Burgundy), France |
| ❊ Pinot Noir | Light-bodied, low tannins, red berries, violets, and earth | Red Burgundy, Pinot Noir, Champagne | Burgundy, Champagne, France; USA (California, Oregon) |
| ❊ Tempranillo | Light- to medium-bodied, low to medium tannins, earthy | Rioja and Ribera del Duero | Rioja and Ribera del Duero, Spain |
| ❊ Sangiovese | Light- to medium-bodied, medium tannins, acidic | Chianti, Sangiovese, Super-Tuscans | Tuscany, Italy |
| ❊ Merlot | Medium- to full-bodied, low to medium tannins, spicy and fruity (plums) | Red Bordeaux, Merlot, "Meritage" wines | Bordeaux, France; USA (California, Washington) |
| ❊ Zinfandel | Medium- to full-bodied, medium to high tannins; berry | Zinfandel | USA (California) |
| ❊ Cabernet Sauvignon | Medium- to full-bodied, high tannins, acidic, black currant | Red Bordeaux, Cabernet Sauvignon, "Meritage" wines | Bordeaux, France; USA (California); Chile |
| ❊ Nebbiolo | Full-bodied, high tannins, roses, violets, tar, truffles, licorice | Barolo and Barbaresco | Piedmont, Italy |
| ❊ Syrah (Shiraz in Australia) | Full-bodied, high tannins, spicy, black pepper | Rhône Valley reds, Shiraz | Rhône Valley, France; Australia |
| ❊ Riesling | Fruity, delicate, acidic, light-bodied | Riesling (some dessert or late harvest) | Alsace, France; Germany; USA (New York and Washington) |
| ❊ Sauvignon Blanc (sometimes called Fumé Blanc in California) | Grassy, herbal, gooseberries, light- to medium-bodied | White Bordeaux, Loire Valley whites (Sancerre, Pouilly-Fumé) | Bordeaux, Loire Valley, France; USA (California); New Zealand |
| ❊ Gewürztraminer | Extremely aromatic and fruity (lychees, mangoes, and roses), spicy | Gewürztraminer | Alsace, France; Germany; Austria |
| ❊ Viognier | Aromatic, very full-bodied, apricots | Viognier or Condrieu | Rhône Valley, France; USA (California) |
| ❊ Chenin Blanc | Fruity, acidic, medium-bodied | Vouvray, Anjou, Saumur | Loire Valley, France; USA (California); South Africa |
| ❊ Chardonnay | Full-bodied, dry (oak gives it buttery, vanilla-y, toasty, oaky flavors) | White Burgundy (Chablis, Macon, Meursault, Pouilly Fuissé), Chardonnay, Champagne | Burgundy, Champagne, France; USA (California); Australia |
| ❊ Melon | Light and almost neutral | Muscadet | Loire Valley, France |
| ❊ Semillon | Alcoholic, full-bodied, low acidity | White Bordeaux, including Sauternes | Bordeaux, France; Australia |
| ❊ Muscat (Moscato in Italian) | Floral, aromatic, sweet | Muscat or Moscato d'Asti, Asti Spumante | Italy, Spain, France |
| ❊ Pinot Gris (Grigio) | Light to medium aromas | Pinot Gris (Grigio) | Alsace, France; Italy; USA (Oregon) |
| ❊ Grüner Veltliner | Aromatic, acidic, spicy, full-bodied | Grüner Veltliner | Austria |
| ❊ Albarino | Aromatic, lemony, and acidic | Albarino | Spain |

# Famous Old World Wines

Since most Old World wine labels do not feature the names of the grape varieties, you'll need to become familiar with the various regions and villages (and even vineyards and châteaux). The chart at right should help you do that. For lack of space, I have included only the most popular wines from the most popular wine-producing Old World countries: France, Italy, and Spain. (Alsace, France, has been omitted since, unlike in the majority of the Old World, Alsatian wine labels feature grape names.)

German and Austrian wines, also not in this table, are mostly white. Ascending levels for German wine include *Kabinett* (light and dry), *Spatlese* (made from later-picked grapes), *Auslese* (made from even later, selectively picked grapes), *Beerenauslese* (made from even later, individually picked grapes), *Trockenbeerenauslese* (made from dried grapes), and *Eiswein* (made from frozen grapes). The last three are dessert wines.

Notice that this table includes the names or types of wines (along with whether they're red or white and what grapes they're made with), as well as—when important—specific villages where they're produced. Beyond the village level, wines can be further designated by individual vineyards or châteaux (just remember that the more details given and the smaller the area, generally the more expensive the wine).

Note: Much of the information from this chart comes from Kevin Zraly's *Windows on the World Complete Wine Course*.

# • FAMOUS OLD WORLD WINES •

## FRANCE

### REGION: BURGUNDY

**Red Burgundy** is made from the Pinot Noir grape. The most famous examples come from the Côte d'Or, which consists of the Côte de Nuits and the Côte de Beaune. In the more prestigious (for red wine) **Côte de Nuits**, look for: **Gevrey-Chambertin, Morey-St-Denis, Chambolle-Musigny, Vougeot Flagey-Echezeaux, Vosne-Romanee,** and **Nuits-St-Georges**. In the **Côte de Beaune**, look for: **Aloxe-Corton, Beaune, Pommard,** and **Volnay**. Key villages in the **Côte Chalonnaise** include **Mercurey, Givry,** and **Rully**.

The best **White Burgundy**, made from the Chardonnay grape, includes **Chablis** (in ascending quality order: **Petit Chablis, Chablis, Chablis Premier Cru, Chablis Grand Cru**); **Maconnais** (generally in ascending quality order: **Mâcon Blanc, Mâcon Superior, Mâcon-Villages, St-Veran, Pouilly-Vinzelles,** and **Pouilly-Fuissé**); **Côte de Beaune** (Aloxe-Corton, Beaune, Meursault, Puligny-Montrachet, and **Chassagne-Montrachet**); and **Côte Chalonnaise** (Montagny and **Rully**).

**Beaujolais** (red), from the Gamay grape, is also produced in this region. In ascending quality order: **Beaujolais** (and **Beaujolais Nouveau**), **Beaujolais-Villages,** and **Beaujolais Cru**.

### REGION: BORDEAUX

The most famous **(Red) Bordeaux** (from Cabernet Sauvignon, Merlot, and Cabernet Franc grapes) comes from: **Médoc (Haut Médoc, St-Estephe, Pauillac, St-Julien, Margaux, Moulis, Listrac); Pomerol; Graves/Pessac-Léognan;** and **St-Emilion**.

**(White) Bordeaux** consists of Sauvignon Blanc and Semillon blends. Generally, white Bordeaux from **Pessac-Léognan** is

a higher quality than wine from **Graves**.

**Sauternes** and **Barsac**, both white dessert wines, are made from Semillon and Sauvignon Blanc grapes; the best wines are made entirely with Semillon.

### REGION: THE LOIRE VALLEY

The Loire produces the following white wines: **Sancerre** (from Sauvignon Blanc), **Pouilly-Fumé** (from Sauvignon Blanc), **Vouvray** (from Chenin Blanc), and **Muscadet** (from Melon).

### REGION: RHÔNE VALLEY

Ascending quality levels in the region are: Côtes du Rhône, Côtes du Rhône Villages, and Côtes du Rhône Crus.

In the **Northern Rhône**, Syrah is primarily used to make the following red wines: **Côte Rôtie, Crozes-Hermitages, Hermitage, St. Joseph,** and **Cornas**.

In the **Southern Rhône**, 13 grapes, including Syrah, Grenache, Mourvedre, and Cinsault, are used to make the following red wines: **Châteauneuf-du-Pape, Côtes du Rhône, Côtes du Rhône-Villages, Côtes du Ventoux, Gigondas,** and **Tavel** (rosé).

### REGION: CHAMPAGNE

**Champagne** is made from Chardonnay, Pinot Noir, and Pinot Meunier grapes. From least to most expensive and exclusive, its categories are: **Nonvintage, NV,** or **MV** (the most popular method, made from a blend of grapes and vintages); **Vintage** (made from grapes from one vintage, only produced in good harvest years); **Blanc de Blancs** (made entirely from Chardonnay grapes); **Rosé** (made with Chardonnay grapes, with a bit of Pinot Noir); and **Luxury Cuvée** (most rare, high-quality bottling, such as Roederer's Cristal and Moët's Dom Perignon). (**Blanc de Noirs** means made entirely with Pinot Noir grapes.) Sweetness categories, from least to most, are: Brut,

Extra Dry, Sec, Demi-Sec, and Doux.

## ITALY

Italy is mostly known for its red wines

### REGION: PIEDMONT

The Piedmont is most famous for the red wines, **Barolo** and **Barbaresco** (both made from the Nebbiolo grape and both better with age).

The Piedmont is also known for its (white) **Moscato d'Asti/Asti Spumante**, (red) **Gattinara**, (red) **Brachetto d'Acqui**, (red) **Ghemme**, and (white) **Gavi**.

### REGION: TUSCANY

Tuscany is most famous for its red **Chianti** (made from Sangiovese and sometimes other grapes), including, in ascending quality order, **Chianti, Chianti Classico,** and **Chianti Classico Riserva**.

Tuscany is also known for its (red) **Brunello di Montalcino**, (white) **Vernaccia di San Gimignano**, and (red) **Vino Nobile di Montepulciano**.

### REGION: THE VENETO

Produces (red) **Valpolicella** (including **Amarone**, made with dried grapes), (red) **Bardolino**, and (white) **Soave**

## SPAIN

The Rioja region is famous for its red wine, **Rioja** (made from Tempranillo and Garnacha grapes), which can be (in ascending quality order), **Crianza, Reserva,** or **Gran Reserva** (5 to 7 years of aging, minimum of 2 years in oak).

Other famous regions include **Ribera del Duero** (which produces reds, primarily from the Tempranillo grape), **Cataluna** (including the Penedes area, which is famous for its sparkling wine, **Cava**), and **Priorato**, where intense reds made primarily from the Garnacha grape are produced. Of course, the area around the town of Jerez (meaning "sherry") is known for its **Sherry**.

# FIND
# YOUR
# WINE

For novices, I recommend beginning with introductory tastings. Start with wines made from popular white grapes (e.g., Chardonnay, Riesling, Sauvignon Blanc, Pinot Gris/Grigio, Gewürztraminer, Viognier). Next, focus on reds, made from popular red grapes (e.g., Pinot Noir, Zinfandel, Merlot, Cabernet Sauvignon, Syrah/Shiraz, and Sangiovese or Nebbiolo). For your third tasting, you can feature less familiar varietals, such as the white grapes Grüner Veltliner (Austria), Semillon (France), Albarino (Spain), Verdejo (Spain), Moscato (Italy), and Chenin Blanc (France).

Once you've gotten to know the key grapes, try featuring wines made with only one type of grape, but from different parts of the world. For example, host an all-Sauvignon Blanc tasting and include Sancerre (from France's Loire Valley), white Bordeaux (admittedly, a blend), and relevant samples from California, Australia, and New Zealand. Or, go with Cabernet Sauvignon and include red Bordeaux (also a blend), and samples from California and Chile, among others.

Or, narrow your focus and only taste wines from a single area, such as Italy, Spain, Bordeaux, or California's Napa Valley. You can also try tasting wines produced by a single vineyard, winemaker, or *négociant* (a wine merchant who purchases grapes or fermented wines, then ages, blends, packages, and sells them under its own name); different vintages of the same wine; different prestige levels of the same type of wine (such as Rioja Crianza, Riserva, and Gran Riserva); or, finally, sparkling, dessert, and fortified wines. If you include both red and white wines, begin by tasting the whites.

## Shopping for Wine

The most important thing you can do when buying wine is to visit the best wine shop you can—save the large discount stores for when you're buying in bulk, purchasing inexpensive wines, or already know exactly which bottles you'd like and are just looking for the most cost-effective source.

Seek out shops with a varied selection, a knowledgeable and helpful staff, and most importantly, proper storage. Bottles should be on their sides, to prevent corks from drying out. The temperature should be consistent and relatively cool, without any direct sunlight on the bottles.

The tannins in red wine are responsible for the red stains red wine leaves on your lips, teeth, and tongue.

Ask the merchant to help you make your selections, giving as many parameters as possible, including your exact price range (don't worry about seeming cheap) and the types of wine you'd like (e.g. white Bordeaux, spicy and full-bodied red wine, or a Chardonnay from California's Napa Valley).

Since you'll most likely be unsure of which vintages are best, ask your merchant to show you a vintage chart. However, unless you're a serious wine connoisseur, don't get too hung up on vintages—the "lesser" vintages are generally less expensive, plus the differences between years usually aren't so obvious, especially to novices.

Further, don't worry too much about experts' ratings; everyone's taste is different and you might not agree with their reviews. As with "good" vintages, highly rated wines are usually more expensive, so unsung (or less lauded) bottles can often be great buys.

You will, however, always want to read the labels carefully and to look for products from reputable wineries (such as Trimbach, in France's Alsace region), *négotiants* (such as Jadot, in France's Burgundy region), or wineries with which you're familiar.

Whichever wines you decide on, ask your merchant to tell you about them, and write down the information in preparation for the tasting. Also ask how best to store and serve the wine, and when to open it—whether immediately or up to ten, or even more, years later (you might not get around to opening it at the tasting!).

Since each tasting portion will only be about 2 (liquid) ounces and the average bottle of wine contains 25 ounces, figure on one bottle of each wine for a tasting of eight to ten people (you will want a bit extra in case your guests would like more).

If you're buying 12 or more bottles, ask if the store can provide a "case" discount (usually 10–15%). Finally, make sure to keep your receipt since, if your wine ends up being corked (spoiled) or is otherwise degraded, you'll want to return it; a reputable store should take back damaged wine.

If you can't find any good local wine shops, try Web sites such as www.sherry-lehmann.com, www.zachys.com, or www.wine.com. Note, however, that some states prohibit the importation of wine.

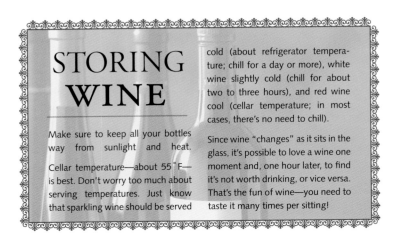

# STORING WINE

Make sure to keep all your bottles away from sunlight and heat.

Cellar temperature—about 55°F—is best. Don't worry too much about serving temperatures. Just know that sparkling wine should be served cold (about refrigerator temperature; chill for a day or more), white wine slightly cold (chill for about two to three hours), and red wine cool (cellar temperature; in most cases, there's no need to chill).

Since wine "changes" as it sits in the glass, it's possible to love a wine one moment and, one hour later, to find it's not worth drinking, or vice versa. That's the fun of wine—you need to taste it many times per sitting!

# CHOOSE YOUR
## ACCOMPANIMENTS

Begin your tasting with some substantial hors d'oeuvres, such as Spinach and Parmigiano-Reggiano Dip (see recipe below) with crudités, Brie en croute (Brie cheese wrapped in puff pastry and baked) with crackers and dried fruit, and a couple of cured sausages, such as saucisson sec. Drink mineral water with citrus slices so that you are sober and alert for the wine tasting.

Pair the wine with plain crackers. Finish with Moscato d'Asti Zabaglione Cream with Fresh Fruit and Biscotti (see recipe on page 37), or poached pears served with Madeleine cookies.

### SPINACH AND PARMIGIANO-REGGIANO DIP

Serve this flavorful, nourishing, quick-to-prepare dip with crudités, such as celery, carrots, and fennel.

Thaw a 10-ounce package of frozen spinach. Then drain and squeeze the spinach dry. Place it in the bowl of a food processor, along with ½ cup of plain whole-milk yogurt, ½ cup of whole-milk sour cream, ¼ teaspoon of ground nutmeg, the freshly grated zest of one lemon, some freshly ground black pepper (about six turns), one large garlic clove, pressed, and ½ teaspoon of coarse or Kosher salt. Puree until well-combined, about 15–20 seconds. Stir in ½ cup of packed, finely grated Parmigiano-Reggiano cheese and serve. This recipe makes about two cups.

# MENU

INTRODUCTION TO RED VARIETALS

(EVENING)

## APPETIZER

SPARKLING AND STILL MINERAL WATER WITH CITRUS SLICES

SPINACH AND PARMIGIANO-REGGIANO DIP WITH CRUDITÉS

BRIE EN CROÛTE WITH DRIED FRUIT AND CRACKERS

CURED SAUSAGES

## TASTING

BEAUJOLAIS (GAMAY GRAPE)

PINOT NOIR

MERLOT

ZINFANDEL

CABERNET SAUVIGNON

SYRAH/SHIRAZ

## ACCOMPANIMENTS

*Plain crackers*

## AFTERWARDS

*Moscato d'Asti Zabaglione Cream with Fresh Fruit and Biscotti*

# MOSCATO D'ASTI ZABAGLIONE CREAM WITH FRESH FRUIT AND BISCOTTI

SERVES 8–10

*If you don't feel like running to the wine shop, Grand Marnier or Marsala can be substituted for the Moscato d'Asti. Note: Since the eggs aren't fully cooked, don't serve this dessert to anyone with a compromised immune system, such as anyone pregnant, very young, or elderly.*

**·1·** Fill a medium-sized pot with a few inches of water. Bring to a simmer and keep over medium heat. Fill a large bowl with ice and cold water and set aside.

**·2·** Meanwhile, in a medium-sized metal bowl, with an electric mixer, beat the egg yolks, sugar, and Moscato d'Asti until well-combined, about 10 seconds.

**·3·** Place the bowl over the pot of simmering water (the bottom of the bowl should not touch the water) and whisk constantly over medium heat until the mixture becomes thick and paler in color, and is 140° F (when measured with an instant-read thermometer), about 5 minutes. (Note: At first, the mixture will be frothy, but it will become more custard-like in consistency as you continue to whisk. Check after 4 minutes, although this process can take up to 7 minutes.)

**·4·** Immediately place the bowl of zabaglione in the bowl of ice water (make sure that no water gets in the custard). Whisking occasionally, let cool, about 3–5 minutes.

**·5·** Meanwhile, with a standing mixer (with the whisk attachment) or an electric mixer, beat the chilled cream at medium-high speed until soft peaks form, about 3 minutes.

**·6·** Using a rubber spatula, gently fold one third of the whipped cream into the room-temperature custard. Fold in another third, then the final third. Cover with plastic wrap and let chill in the refrigerator for at least 30 minutes, or up to 1 day.

**·7·** When ready to serve, divide the fruit among 8–10 parfait or martini glasses or glass bowls. Top with dollops of the zabaglione and serve with biscotti.

Zabaglione:

8 egg yolks
(from large eggs)

½ cup granulated sugar

½ cup Moscato d'Asti
(or another Muscat
grape-based sweet wine)

1½ cups heavy
cream, chilled

Accompaniments:

About 6 cups prepared
fresh fruit, such a mangoes,
berries, peaches, plums,
bananas, pineapples,
oranges, seedless red
grapes, kiwis, or pears
(include either 1 type of
fruit or a combination)

8–10 small biscotti (try
to find a flavored variety,
such as cranberry-orange)

# ORGANIZE YOUR
# TASTING

Consider having your wine tasting after dinner; you could even serve sweet wines with desserts. Or have a wine tasting in lieu of a traditional cocktail party. Whatever you choose, here's how to get acquainted with this earthy, yet sophisticated beverage.

## WHAT YOU'LL NEED

Before conducting the tasting, make sure to have on hand "The Basics" (see Chapter 1), as well as the materials below. Before the tasting, make sure your wineglasses are very clean and do not bear any soap residue or aromas. Line the wine bottles up in the order in which you'll be trying them, from lightest- to fullest-bodied, driest to sweetest, and white to red (if these conflict, the last rule should take precedence).

During the tasting, pour about 2 ounces of each wine into each person's glass (the average regular pour is five to six ounces, or about a third of a glassful). Do not rinse glasses between samples, as any residual water can dilute the wines. Just make sure to discard unwanted wine (into the bucket) before pouring the next sample.

### MATERIALS

Appropriate wines

Corkscrew (experts recommend the Screwpull® or waiter's-style)

White napkins, at least one for each guest (for gauging wine color)

Wineglasses (one for each guest)

Bucket or large bowl, in the center of the table

Accompaniments, including neutral-flavored white crackers

# LEARN YOUR
# PALATE

- •1• Hold the first glass up at a 45-degree angle against a white napkin. How would you describe the wine's color? Does it look saturated or watery? (Remember that older wines can look brown.)

- •2• Now, put the glass down on the table and swirl it vigorously, to release the wine's aromas. Then bring the glass up to your nose and inhale deeply. How would you describe the aromas? Are they subtle or strong?

- •3• Now, take a sip of the wine and swish it all around the inside of your mouth, taking care not to swallow. You can also take in some air (to release more aromas and flavors). Consider the wine's flavors, acidity (sometimes called "crispness"), and sweetness (most wines are dry). You want these elements to be in balance.

- •4• For red wines, what is the tannin level? (Tannin comes across as a velvety or scratchy, drying mouthfeel, similar to over-steeped black tea. The tannins should be in balance with the other elements.) What about the wine's body? Is it light, or very full and almost heavy? What about the wine's alcohol level? (Wine with a high level of alcohol can seem very soft and a bit sweet or—if the amount is extremely high—even bitter.)

- •5• Swallow the wine and consider its finish or aftertaste. Is it long or short, meaning does it last a while or instantly dissipate? (A long finish is considered superior.) Is the wine complex, meaning does it have depth, or more than just one layer of flavor?

- •6• Finally—and most importantly—do you like the wine?

# TASTING GRID

As you taste each wine, write the answers to the questions on page 40 on a copy of this grid. Feel free to use the tasting terms provided below, and keep the grid as a record of your favorite wines.

| | ·1· | ·2· | ·3· | ·4· | ·5· | ·6· |
|---|---|---|---|---|---|---|
| **WINE NAME** | | | | | | |
| **COLOR AND INTENSITY** *Color: pale yellow, yellow-green, gold, ruby red, deep purple, garnet. Saturation: high or low.* | | | | | | |
| **AROMA** *Strong or mild; apple, pear, peach, lemon, mango, blueberry, black currant, strawberry, cherry, fig, raisin, tart, sweet, herbal, grass, green pepper, caramel, tobacco, leather, mineral, earth.* | | | | | | |
| **FLAVOR, ACIDITY, SWEETNESS** *Flavor: see "aroma." Acidity: high or low. Sweetness: high or low. Balance?* | | | | | | |
| **TANNINS, BODY, ALCOHOL** *Tannins: high or low. Body/Texture: thick or thin. Alcohol level: high or low.* | | | | | | |
| **FINISH AND COMPLEXITY** *Finish: long or short. Complexity: multidimensional or straightforward.* | | | | | | |
| **DO YOU LIKE IT?** | | | | | | |

# WINE

**American Viticultural Area (AVA) and Appellation:** Designated or recognized wine-growing area (the first term is used in the United States; the second in France).

**Brix:** A measurement of the sugar in grapes (it increases as grapes ripen).

**Corked:** Wine whose corks have been tainted by naturally occurring chemicals; corked wines have wet cardboard-like aromas.

**Cru (Grand Cru and Premier Cru):** French term referring to grapes from the best plots of land and the best vintages (Grand is the highest, followed by Premier, and Cru); these wines are pricey and prestigious.

**Dry (and Off-dry, Medium-dry):** Not sweet (off-dry is slighter sweeter, while medium-dry is still sweeter, although none are truly sweet).

**Estate-bottled:** Wines for which one entity was responsible for both the viticulture and vinification.

**Lees (and Sur Lees):** Yeast solids, over which some wines age for complex, not-fruity aromas and flavors.

**Nose:** Aromas of a wine.

**Reserve or Riserva:** Denotes a higher status of wine; regulated in some countries (Spain, Italy) and not in others (the United States).

**Residual Sugar:** Sugar left over in the wine after fermentation.

**Suss-Reserve:** German phrase meaning adding unfermented grape juice to wine to sweeten it.

**Tannins:** Mouth-drying substances present in grape skins, seeds, and stems, as well as in oak barrels; a key characteristic of red wine, and a preservative.

**Terroir:** Particular characteristics of specific pieces of land, encompassing soil, elevation, and climate.

**Varietal:** Wine made primarily from one variety of grape, such as Syrah/Shiraz.

**Vintage:** Year in which the grapes were harvested.

# CHOCOLATE

---

*chapter three*

You may not be surprised to learn that chocolate's botanical name, *Theobroma cacao*, means "food of the gods." A heavenly food indeed, with its velvety-smooth mouthfeel and rich, intense flavor. Nothing compares.

Not only does chocolate taste great—it also contains natural stimulants that make you feel happy, energized, and in love. Perhaps that's why Napoleon regularly consumed chocolate on his military campaigns, Madame du Barry asked her lovers to drink chocolate before visiting, and Casanova considered chocolate more of an aphrodisiac than champagne.

Even better—chocolate is good for you! Chocolate contains antioxidants, which, according to several scientific studies, may help prevent cancer. Buoyed by this research, I try to have chocolate every single day, most often in my healthy (and not so healthy) version of hot chocolate (you'll find the recipes on page 61).

# KNOW YOUR CHOCOLATE

Given all the benefits of chocolate, you may be tempted to run out and buy a monster bar at the grocery store. But, before you clean out the Winn-Dixie, know that the best type for your health is premium quality bittersweet. Far more intense than the mass-market brands we all know and love, it is closer to the source of all things chocolate: the cocoa bean.

## MEET THE COCOA BEAN

Cocoa beans grow in pods on cocoa trees, which flourish within 20 degrees north and south of the equator—in Africa, South America, Mexico, the Caribbean, and Indonesia. The pods look like large, almond-shaped squash and are roughly the size of footballs. Ranging in color from lemon yellow to green, orange, red, and purple, they contain a sweet white pulp, as well as 35 to 40 small beans. It takes about 400 of these beans to make just one pound of chocolate!

Despite the wide variety of pods, every cocoa tree and bean falls into one of three varieties: *forastero, criollo*, or *trinitario*. Forasteros (with the exception of the *arriba* bean from Ecuador) are the least expensive, hardiest, and most common type of bean. They also tend to be incredibly bitter. Nonetheless, with the addition of sugar, they form the base for most inexpensive chocolate. At the other end of the spectrum are criollos, the most expensive, delicate, and rare type of bean. In the middle lie trinitarios, which are a hybrid of forasteros and criollos.

Since the time of the Aztecs and Mayans, most chocolate has been made from a blend of all three types of beans. In fact, unless the package says otherwise, you can assume that a chocolate product is a blend, or *cuvée*. Typically, cuvée bars are made primarily from the cheaper, "bulk" forasteros, with the more expensive "flavor" criollo and trinitario beans added in much smaller quantities.

Nonetheless, in recent years, mounting consumer interest in the sources of foods has led many upscale and boutique companies to produce chocolate using only one type of bean, or beans from a single region or country. The former is known as single variety chocolate, while the latter is referred to as single origin (estate-grown, single-estate, or single-plantation describes chocolates whose beans hail from only one plantation or estate).

⌘

*According to a study, cocoa powder contains more heart-healthy antioxidants than many other chocolate products. Why does chocolate melt in our mouths and not in our hands? Cocoa butter's melting point is just below human body temperature.*

⌘

Although these high-end chocolates have become trendy, they are not necessarily superior to blended bars—they're just different. Overall, if you prefer a more mellow, balanced flavor—such as traditional Belgian chocolate—opt for a cuvée. If, on the other hand, you like your chocolate intense and deep in flavor (and are interested in venturing closer to the beans from which it was made), try a single origin or single variety bar.

## The Story of Chocolate, from Bean to Bar

In their natural form, cocoa beans neither look nor taste like chocolate. Each one consists of a hard hull or kernel containing cocoa nibs (brown solids that give chocolate its color and flavor) and cocoa butter. The cocoa butter is a fat whose content fluctuates with the seasons, but ranges from about 46–61% of the bean. There is no sugar in a cocoa bean.

So how do we get from these beans to the chocolate bar? First, the pods are picked and opened. Then, the seeds and sugary pulp are removed and covered with leaves. During a two- to six-day fermentation period, the sugars in the pulp help reduce the acidity of the beans and develop their flavor and color. Under-fermenting can preserve too much undesirable acidic flavor, while over-fermenting can make the beans taste like rotten fruit. Once fermented, the beans are dried in the sun for about five days before being sorted and shipped.

At the factory, the now smaller and darker beans are roasted for between thirty minutes and two hours to heighten their flavor. Under-roasting results in a lack of flavor, while over-roasting can cause bitterness (just like over-roasting nuts in your oven). (Often, mediocre beans are roasted for a longer period of time, since roasting can disguise their lackluster flavors.) Next, the outer skins are removed and the nibs are broken down with stones or disks. The heat from this process liquefies the nibs, causing them to form a thick, dark-brown paste called *chocolate liquor*. This liquor is then further refined by rollers, which decrease the size of its particles.

According to lore, a worker in a London trading house incorrectly spelled "cacao" "cocoa." The new name stuck. Now, cacao is often used to refer to the raw material, while cocoa refers to finished products, such as cocoa powder.

If the pure chocolate liquor is placed in molds, it becomes unsweetened, or baking, chocolate (when all of the remaining cocoa butter is extracted from the liquor, unsweetened cocoa powder is produced). To make eating chocolate, manufacturers add sugar and vanilla (or artificial vanillin) to the chocolate liquor. Next, the mixture is refined and *conched* (vigorously whipped) for anywhere from four hours to several days to remove excess moisture and acid, and to achieve a smooth texture. Too much conching can cause blandness, while too little conching can leave the chocolate overly acidic.

Finally, additional cocoa butter and an emulsifier, such as the soy by-product, lecithin, are added to render the chocolate smooth and shiny. The chocolate is then tempered (warmed, stirred, and cooled for a smooth, glossy, crisp finish), molded, fully cooled, and wrapped. *Voilà*—chocolate.

## FOUR TYPES OF CHOCOLATE?

But, what about dark (bittersweet and semi-sweet), milk, and white chocolate? Bittersweet chocolate contains the least sugar, followed by semisweet. Those who love black coffee will most likely flock to bittersweet chocolate, while those who prefer a slightly softer bite will generally prefer semisweet. Milk chocolate, the mildest in flavor, possesses even more sugar than semisweet (as well as milk by-products).

White chocolate, since it does not contain chocolate liquor or cocoa solids (the ground nibs that lend chocolate its color and flavor), is not really chocolate at all. It's a mixture of milk, sugar, vanilla, an emulsifier, and cocoa butter or vegetable fat. (When shopping for white chocolate, look for an ivory color, which reveals the use of cocoa butter, rather than less expensive vegetable fat.)

> " When my father told me about big, strange-looking fruits that sprouted right out of the tree bark and were filled with beans that are the source of all chocolate, I formed " a mental picture of thick-skinned papayas full of fragrant Hershey's chocolate kisses.
>
> —*The New Taste of Chocolate*, Maricel E. Presilla

## DECIPHERING THE LABEL

Believe it or not, chocolate isn't always manna from heaven—and it's difficult to separate the wheat from the chaff when confronted with a bevy of labels, most of which reveal little about product quality. That being said, you can determine a bit about a bar's pedigree by reading the wrapper.

First, the quality of a bar depends largely on the quality of the beans from which it was produced. Criollos and trinitarios are generally superior to forasteros, largely because they are less bitter. Look for either of those terms, or arriba (the only superior-quality Forastero bean) on the label. Also look for information about where the beans grew, ideally the specific regions, or even particular estates or plantations. A printed date of harvest or production is always a plus—although dark chocolate can be stored for up to a year, the quality definitely doesn't increase as it ages.

It's also key that chocolatiers combine the beans with the right balance of natural ingredients. Look for natural vanilla, as opposed to vanillin, on the list of ingredients, and opt for products with 32–39% cocoa butter, which ensures a fluid texture.

## TRENDS IN CHOCOLATE

Although all chocolate is made in basically the same way, there are a number of exciting developments occurring all around us. For one, production of organic and fair-trade bars is growing (fair trade means that exporters share more of the profits with farmers). Also hot are boutique chocolatiers, which produce creative, high-quality, all-natural chocolates in small numbers and designer flavors, such as Szechuan pepper, green tea ginger, or Earl Grey chocolate.

Even more importantly, consider the cacao (or cocoa) content. The higher the percentage, the more intense the cocoa flavor and bitter the bar—dark chocolate typically contains at least 35% cacao content, but premium brands (such as Valrhona) produce bars with 70% or more. (It's difficult to mask the quality of the beans when the cacao content is high; thus, a high percentage usually means a good product.)

Mass-market bars generally don't specify their cocoa content; but, you can assume that it will be low. If a bar has a higher cocoa content, like Lindt's "Excellence Dark" (at 85%), it will have smaller quantities of other ingredients, such as sugar, and, hence, will taste quite bitter.

# FIND YOUR
# CHOCOLATE

Since most people are familiar with the taste differences between dark, milk, and white chocolates, I would stick with one general category, such as dark, when tasting.

I personally favor focusing on bittersweet chocolate—specifically, plain bittersweet chocolate bars. That way, you can really get in touch with the flavor of the bean, rather than that of sugar, milk, or flavorings. (See the Dark Chocolate Menu on page 58.) However, if you prefer milder chocolate, consider conducting a tasting of semisweet or milk varieties—it's completely up to you and your taste buds.

In order to keep things interesting, aim for variety within the category you've chosen. This generally means a combination of single-origin, single-variety, and cuveé bars. It's also fun to include one chocolate with a lower cacao content, such as the Cote d'Or "Noir de Noir" (with 56% cacao) to experience the difference. (If you're used to milder chocolate, you'll likely prefer this sample.)

Whatever you choose, try to include the highest-quality products possible. You can usually count on high-end manufacturers to make extremely high-caliber chocolate. Premium-quality chocolate is never cheap, although the best is not necessarily the most expensive. Six products should make for a comprehensive, thought not overwhelming, tasting.

## SHOPPING FOR CHOCOLATE

Order enough chocolate so that each participant has a total of 2½ ounces. You can purchase high-quality chocolate at your nearest

gourmet food shop or through online merchants like www.chocosphere.com, www.chocolatetradingco.com, and www.chocolatesource.com. (Other Web sources include www.echocolates.com and www.formaggio-kitchen.com.) If you're having the products shipped during the warmer months, opt for warm-weather shipping, which will prevent melting. The extra cost is usually about $10 and definitely worth it.

Although flavored chocolates are delicious, I wouldn't include them in a tasting. You want to focus on the chocolate itself, and not on the flavorings, which can often dominate a bar's character. But, for a special treat afterward, consider ordering flavored chocolates from www.vosgeschocolate.com. The company's "Black Pearl" (with Japanese ginger, wasabi, black sesame seeds, and dark chocolate), "Barcelona" (with hickory-smoked almonds, *fleur de sel* gray sea salt, and dark milk chocolate), and "Naga" (with sweet Indian curry powder, coconut flakes, and milk chocolate) are truly a revelation! Other sites for good-quality flavored chocolate are www.johnandkiras.com and www.lamaisonduchocolat.com.

# STORING CHOCOLATE

Moisture, light, and heat are chocolate's worst enemies. So, once you've received your chocolate, make sure to wrap it tightly and to store it in a dry, cool, dark place (preferably between 45–60°F). Do not refrigerate. Dark chocolate should last for up to one year, milk chocolate for six months, and white chocolate for three months. If the temperature changes or the chocolate has not been well tempered, a pale gray "bloom," or surface streaks and blotches, may appear. What you're seeing is butter rising to the surface. In damp conditions, tiny gray sugar crystals can appear as well. In both cases, the chocolate is still edible—enjoy!

## MELTING LEFTOVER CHOCOLATE

To melt chocolate, first chop or break it into small pieces—a serrated or chef's knife, or even your hands, will do. Exercise caution when melting, as chocolate can scorch easily: If using the stovetop, place the chocolate in a heat-proof bowl over a pot of simmering water (the bottom of the bowl shouldn't touch the water). Stir until the chocolate melts, about three minutes. Alternatively, place the chocolate in a microwave-safe bowl and heat over high for 30 seconds. Remove from the microwave, stir, then heat in 20-second increments, stirring each time, until the chocolate has melted. Whatever the method, make sure that no droplets of water come in contact with the chocolate (they can cause it to become lumpy or grainy).

Despite conceptions to the contrary, chocolate is not high in caffeine. One cup of hot cocoa has the same amount as a cup of decaffeinated coffee: about 5 milligrams. Meanwhile, according to www.hersheys.com, Hershey's 1.45-ounce "Special Dark Chocolate Bar" contains 31 milligrams, while the 1.55-ounce Hershey's "Chocolate Bar" (milk chocolate) has 9 milligrams.

# CHOOSE YOUR
## ACCOMPANIMENTS

Begin your tasting with a glass of sparkling wine, such as Prosecco or Cava, as well as sweet and salty appetizers. Consider Croutes with Blue Cheese, Toasted Walnuts, and a Port Wine Reduction (see page 60) or Dates Stuffed with Gorgonzola, Bacon, and Chives (see page 59). Alongside, set out cheeses and crackers (I love to serve Spanish varieties, such as Manchego and Zamorano, with quince paste). Alternatively, you can try wrapping fresh figs or melon slices with prosciutto or tossing watermelon cubes with sea salt, lime juice, and chili powder.

Serve sliced baguette with the chocolate (one baguette should suffice for up to eight tasters). If you like, you can also offer dessert wine, such as Port, Muscat, Sauternes, or Tokaji. For fun, pour glasses of two types of dessert wine for trying with the different chocolates, and determine which wine you prefer with which chocolate. In this way, you will get to know dessert wines a little better, too—and I can't think of anything wrong with that. Chocolate tastings are all about decadence.

Cleanse your palate with water (and bread) in between chocolates. After the tasting, bring out a bowl of fresh fruit, such as clementines or pineapple chunks (the acidity will help to refresh the palate).

In ancient Mayan society, new couples shared a beverage made with cacao, water, vanilla, black pepper, and other spices at betrothal and marriage ceremonies.

# MENU

DARK CHOCOLATE TASTING
(EVENING)

## APPETIZER

CAVA

DATES STUFFED WITH GORGONZOLA, BACON, AND CHIVES

MANCHEGO AND ZAMORANO CHEESES WITH MEMBRILLO
(QUINCE PASTE) AND OLIVE OIL SEA SALT CRACKERS

## TASTING

CÔTE D'OR "NOIR DE NOIR" *Belgian, cuvée, 56% cacao*

EL REY "GRAN SAMAN" *Venezuelan, single origin, 70% cacao*

CHOCOVIC "GUARANDA" *Spanish, single origin, 71% minimum cacao*

VALRHONA "GUANAJA" *French, cuvée, 70% cacao*

SCHARFFEN BERGER "BITTERSWEET CHOCOLATE BAR" *American, cuvée, 70% cacao*

MICHEL CLUIZEL "1ER CRU DE PLANTATION 'MARALUMI'
DARK CHOCOLATE BAR" *French, single-plantation, 64% cacao*

## ACCOMPANIMENT

*Baguette*

## AFTERWARDS

*Clementines*

# RECIPES FOR ACCOMPANIMENTS

Choose one of the following hors d'oeuvres to have before the tasting—blue cheese is a wonderfully salty prelude to chocolate, hence the inclusion of two such recipes. Keep in mind that the Port Reduction on page 60, intended here for drizzling over the croutes, is also delicious served with a wedge of blue cheese.

## DATES STUFFED WITH GORGONZOLA, BACON, AND CHIVES

### (MAKES 44, SERVES 12)

*Feel free to prepare this sweet, salty, and smoky hors d'oeuvre several hours ahead—just cover and refrigerate, bringing to room temperature before serving. Leftovers are good for up to two days, if tightly covered and chilled. Inspired by a recipe in* **Martha Stewart Living**.

•1• Arrange the date halves on a platter, spreading them open with your fingers.

•2• Place the bacon in a cold small- to- medium skillet (nonstick is helpful). Turn the heat to medium-high and cook until slightly brown and crisp, turning over after 2–4 minutes, a total of 5–8 minutes. Transfer to a plate covered with a few paper towels and let cool for 5 minutes. Place on a cutting board and, with a chef's knife, cut into very small pieces (the diced bacon should add up to about 2 tablespoons plus 1 teaspoon).

•3• In a medium bowl, mix the cheese with the bacon, black pepper, and chives until well-incorporated and the cheese softens. Transfer into a pastry bag or large freezer bag. If the latter, spoon the mixture into one corner. Then twist the bag, further squeezing the mixture into that corner. Cut a quarter-inch or so off of that bottom corner. Using the filled bag, pipe the mixture onto each date half. (Alternatively, just use a spoon.) Garnish with additional chives and serve.

22 large, soft dried dates, halved lengthwise and pitted

2 strips bacon (such as Niman Ranch)

8 ounces Gorgonzola Dolce or another soft blue cheese, such as Maytag Blue, at room temperature for 30 minutes

Freshly ground black pepper to taste (about 4 grinds)

2 teaspoons minced fresh chives, plus another teaspoon for garnish

## CROÛTES WITH BLUE CHEESE, TOASTED WALNUTS, AND A PORT WINE REDUCTION

(MAKES 16, SERVES 8)

*Feel free to substitute a strong honey, such as chestnut, or even Balsamic Reduction (see page 85), for the Port Reduction. You may also substitute caramelized onions for the walnuts and a baguette for the ciabatta.*

- •1• Preheat oven to 350°F. When preheated, place bread slices on one baking sheet and the nuts on another, and bake until both are golden brown and aromatic, about 10 minutes. (Start checking the nuts after 5 minutes, to prevent them from burning.)

- •2• Remove both trays from the oven. Spread the cheese evenly over each piece of bread and return the toasts to the oven until the cheese melts, about 5 minutes.

- •3• Remove the cheese toasts from the oven and sprinkle evenly with the walnuts. Drizzle with the Port Reduction and serve immediately.

1 ciabatta, cut on the bias into 16 slices, each ½-inch-thick

½ cup finely chopped walnuts

¾ cup soft blue cheese (such as Gorgonzola Dolce or Saga Blue)

1 tablespoon plus 1 teaspoon Port Reduction (see below)

## PORT WINE REDUCTION

(MAKES ABOUT ½ CUP)

*Drizzle this syrup over blue cheeses and their accompaniments. Use an inexpensive Port, since you'll be cooking it down. Feel free to make this up to 1 week in advance (store in a tightly sealed container).*

- •1• Pour 2 cups of Port into a small, heavy saucepan. Bring to a boil, then reduce to a simmer over medium-low heat. Keep watching the pot, as the Port can burn. Simmer 15–20 minutes (less if you prefer a thinner reduction, more if you prefer a syrup).

# Recipes for Hot Chocolate

Hot chocolate is *so* divine that I've given you two recipes,
one perfectly sinful and one for the health-conscious.

## DINA'S DECIDEDLY DEVILISH HOT CHOCOLATE

(SERVES 2 OR UP TO 4 IF YOU PREFER SMALLER PORTIONS)

*This thick, sinful hot chocolate is the perfect vehicle for leftover chocolate pieces. But
beware: it's extremely rich! Keep in mind that, depending on the chocolate you use,
you might need to add sugar to taste. For variations, feel free to add almond extract to
simulate Mexican chocolate. Or, for a winter treat, replace the espresso powder and vanilla
extract with mint extract, and serve with a peppermint stick (rather than a cinnamon stick).*

•1• In a heavy, medium-sized saucepan over medium-high heat, bring milk, with salt, to a simmer. Immediately remove from the heat and add chocolate, cocoa powder, vanilla, and espresso, if using. Whisk vigorously until smooth.

•2• Ladle the hot chocolate into mugs. If you like, garnish with cinnamon sticks, freshly whipped cream, and chocolate shavings.

2 cups skim milk (trust me: whole milk or cream would be excessive!)

1/8 teaspoon table or iodized salt

1/2 cup, packed finely chopped, bittersweet chocolate (try a mix of your leftovers, such as Valrhona and Scharffen-Berger)

1/2 cup semisweet chocolate chips (such as Ghiradelli)

1 tablespoon unsweetened cocoa powder

1 teaspoon pure vanilla extract

Optional: 1/8 teaspoon espresso powder, 2 cinnamon sticks, freshly whipped cream, chocolate shavings

## DINA'S (ALMOST) ANGELIC HOT CHOCOLATE

(SERVES 2)

*This hot chocolate is healthful enough to drink every day—seriously!
If you use another brand of vanilla-flavored soy milk for this recipe,
you'll probably need to adjust the amount of seasoning and sugar.*

•1• Over medium-high heat in a heavy, medium-sized saucepan, bring soy milk to a simmer with cinnamon sticks and salt. Then immediately remove from the heat and add cocoa powder, vanilla, and sugar. Whisk until very smooth, ladle into mugs, and serve.

3 cups vanilla-flavored soy milk (preferably the Silk brand)

2 cinnamon sticks

1/4 teaspoon table or iodized salt

1/2 cup unsweetened cocoa powder

1 teaspoon pure vanilla extract

3 tablespoons granulated or white sugar

# ORGANIZE YOUR
# TASTING

Set out six plates along the center of your table. Carefully unwrap the first chocolate, placing its label in front of the first plate (this label will identify the chocolate). Alternatively, use index cards to make labels for each chocolate, but save the wrappers anyway— your guests will probably want to see them. Place the bar(s) on a cutting board and break into roughly 1-inch-square pieces (make sure there is at least one piece of each type of chocolate for each guest). If you've purchased a large block of chocolate that's too difficult to break up with your hands, use a serrated or chef's knife or a cleaver to chop it into pieces. In order to form squares rather than thin shards, bear down hard on the chocolate with the bottom third of your knife, pressing on the top of the blade with your other hand. Place the pieces from the first chocolate on the first plate. Repeat the steps above until you've chopped and distributed all six kinds of chocolate. (If you cover the plates with plastic wrap, you can do this up to four hours in advance.)

## WHAT YOU'LL NEED

Before the tasting, make sure to have on hand "The Basics" (see Chapter 1), as well as the materials at right, and any accompaniments you decide to serve.

### MATERIALS
Cutting board

6 plates and appropriate chocolates

A platter and baguette slices

# LEARN YOUR
# PALATE

·1· Examine the chocolate and describe its appearance. Keep in mind that color, patterning, and shape aren't significant. Instead, ask yourself whether the bar is glossy and dry—both signs demonstrating proper tempering technique (meaning the warming, stirring, and cooling of the chocolate to establish the correct appearance and consistency). Now, break a piece of the chocolate in two—a product that breaks cleanly has also been well-tempered.

·2· Rub the sample between your fingers, placing it in front of your nose and covering it with your other hand. Close your eyes, inhale for a few seconds, and consider its aroma.

·3· Place the chocolate on your tongue, close your eyes, and let the chocolate melt for about 30 seconds—don't bite down, though. Spread the chocolate all over your tongue and the roof of your mouth. Consider its flavor and texture (the latter is known as *mouthfeel*).

·4· Bite down on the chocolate and chew a few times. Keep your eyes closed and determine how the flavor has changed. Has it gotten stronger, sweeter, more flavorful, more bitter? What flavor notes do you detect now? Has the texture changed?

·5· Swallow the chocolate and reflect on its finish (or aftertaste). Is it long or short, meaning do the flavors dissipate quickly or last for a while in your mouth? (Note: A long finish is considered desirable.) What flavors remain?

·6· Do you like the chocolate?

# TASTING GRID

As you taste each chocolate, write your answers to the questions on the previous page on a copy of the below grid. Feel free to use the examples of tasting terms given below, and keep a record of the grid for future purchases.

| | ·1· | ·2· | ·3· | ·4· | ·5· | ·6· |
|---|---|---|---|---|---|---|
| **CHOCOLATE NAME** | | | | | | |
| **APPEARANCE** *Glossy, dry, clean breakage?* | | | | | | |
| **AROMA** *Positive: fruit, coffee, floral, nuts, caramel, spicy. Negative: burnt rubber, plastic, smoky, rotten fruit, stale.* | | | | | | |
| **FLAVOR** *Positive: subtle acidity and sweetness, balanced. Negative: acrid, intensely bitter, extremely acidic, overly sweet, not sweet enough. Other descriptors: nuts, caramel, toffee, fruit, vanilla, tobacco, smoke, salt, raisins, red wine, cinnamon, black pepper, flowers, mild, strong,* | | | | | | |
| **TEXTURE** *Positive: firm, effortless melt. Negative: sticky, waxy, sandy, or grainy. Other descriptors: smooth, creamy, velvety, hard, chalky, dry, light, heavy, thick.* | | | | | | |
| **FINISH** *Long or short? Aftertaste: bitter, sweet, strong, mild.* | | | | | | |
| **DO YOU LIKE IT?** | | | | | | |

# CHOCOLATE
## glossary

**Cocoa Content** (or **Cocoa Solids**): Percentage of the bar containing cocoa butter and chocolate liquor from ground nibs. The higher the number, the less diluted (and generally more intense) the chocolate.

**Cuvée:** Chocolates composed of a blend of beans. Unless the package says otherwise, assume that a chocolate is a cuvée.

**Dark Chocolate:** Chocolate whose cocoa (solids) content ranges from 35–100%; encompasses unsweetened/bitter/baking, bittersweet, and semisweet chocolate. Dark chocolates are less sweet and more bitter than milk or white chocolate.

**Estate-Grown:** Chocolates whose beans hail from only one plantation or estate.

**Fair Trade:** The practice whereby exporters share more of their profits with farmers.

**Milk Chocolate:** Sweet and mild, milk chocolate contains at least 10% chocolate liquor, as well as sugar, vanilla (or vanillin), lecithin, and at least 12% milk solids.

**Single Origin:** Chocolates whose beans hail from only one region or country.

**Single Variety:** Chocolates made from one type of bean (e.g., Porcelana, a type of criollo).

**White Chocolate:** Although good-quality brands contain cocoa butter, white chocolate is not real chocolate because it does not include cocoa nibs. As with milk chocolate, white chocolate contains dairy by-products.

# CHEESE

*chapter four*

By turns rich and unctuous, nutty and flaky, or moist and crumbly, cheese is all things to all people. So, it's easy to forget that, in essence, it's nothing but coagulated milk. For something so fundamentally simple, cheese has played an instrumental role in human history: in times of scarcity, the concentrated form of protein offered sustenance—not something we consider when browning a grilled cheese sandwich or laying out a cheese platter for a cocktail party.

Cheese is particularly appropriate for entertaining because of its variety. There really is a cheese for everyone—it's just a matter of discovering your own personal preference. The problem is how to go about doing that. Most of us have blinders on when it comes to cheese. Although aware of the Big 10 (Cheddar, Gouda, Parmigiano-Reggiano, mozzarella, feta, Brie, Camembert, Muenster, blue, and perhaps ricotta), we may be intimidated by all the others. It's always easier to stick with the familiar, but cheese offers such ample rewards that it's worth venturing into unknown territory.

# KNOW YOUR
# CHEESE

Who would think that humble milk—partner to peanut butter sandwiches and chocolate chip cookies—was capable of being spun into so many euphoria-inducing cheeses? Talk about potential!

It all starts with the milking of the cows, goats, sheep, or other animals (believe it or not, the best mozzarella is made from the milk of water buffaloes!). In some cases, the milk comes from the same farm that makes the cheeses (these highly esteemed products are known as *farmstead, farmhouse,* or *fermière* cheeses). Most of the time, though, the milk is transported from farms to cheesemakers. Sometimes, cheesemakers cull milk from surrounding farms only, producing a local type of cheese; Italy's famed Parmigiano-Reggiano is an example of this. Other times, milk comes from a mixture of dairies, and production is larger in scale.

Regardless of the type of animal and farm from which it comes, all milk consists of two principal parts: solids, and a liquid known as *whey*. To make most kinds of cheese, milk is warmed and then treated with a starter culture—usually strains of bacteria, but sometimes fermented whey from the previous day. The starter converts the *lactose* (or milk sugar) into lactic acid, beginning the coagulation of the milk (the process by which the solids become curds). An enzyme called *rennet* (most often from calf stomachs) is then added to continue the coagulation process.

Once a sufficient number of curds have formed and reached the correct level of acidity, they are usually stirred and cut up. The larger the pieces, the softer the cheese (large curds contain more water, hence they result in a moister end product).

After cutting the curds, the cheesemaker drains them of whey and places them in molds (the more whey that is removed, the denser the cheese). At this point, many cheeses are pressed, and then salted, either through dry-rubbing or by being immersed in brine. Salt expedites the drying process, adds flavor, and hinders the formation of undesirable bacteria. Another benefit of salt is that it helps the cheese form a rind. In some cases, cheesemakers will assist in the rind formation process by exposing their product to mold (such as *Penicillium candidum* for Brie cheese). Other times, they'll "wash" their cheese in liquids, such as wine, grape brandy, brine, or cider.

> Cheese is about 1/10th the volume of the milk from which it was made.

Whether they've formed a rind or not, most cheeses are set aside in humid, cool areas to age, although a few are sold fresh. The longer a cheese ages, the drier and more concentrated in flavor it becomes; some Cheddars, for example, can age for as long as six years.

## MILK MATTERS

Even more than bacteria, good cheese requires good milk. In fact, much of what we identify with cheese is determined by the source material. It all begins with the type of animal producing the milk: cow, goat (chèvre), sheep (ewe), yak, camel, water buffalo, reindeer, mare, or some combination (cow, goat, and sheep are the most common).

Sheep's milk is buttery (with the highest concentration of solids and fat), while goat's milk is pure white, lighter-bodied, a bit chalky, piquant, and mineral-rich in taste. Sweet, slightly acidic cow's milk falls somewhere between the two. You'll also notice that some cheeses are described as "skimmed," meaning that the cream was skimmed off the top of the milk before the curds formed. In contrast, cream is added to triple crèmes, such as Pierre Robert and Explorateur, both similar to Brie.

*Terroir* (pronounced ter-wahr)—or the land on which the animal grazed—is also a crucial determinant of the character of the cheese. The more varied and healthy the plant material, the more interesting the resulting milk. That's why, in the summer, some farmers change the scenery by leading their animals to the uplands, or *alpage*, where they dine on a smorgasbord of plants and herbs (this age-old practice of moving the herd is called transhumance).

In the spring and early fall, new grass grows, creating what many consider to be the most flavorful milk and tastiest cheeses. In winter, many animals generally feed on hay, resulting in whiter and less interesting cheese.

Unfortunately, it's not always obvious which season a cheese came from. Depending on the length of the aging process, a "summer" cheese could be available in summer, fall, winter, or even spring. To avoid confusion, just ask your cheesemonger which products have been made from "spring" and "early fall" milk.

## PASTEURIZED OR RAW? RIPE OR FRESH?

Invented by the Frenchman Louis Pasteur in the second half of the 19th century, pasteurization is the process of heating milk to a high temperature to kill off bacteria. This sounds like a good idea, except that bacteria are the primary sources of cheese flavor and character. With a few exceptions, cheese made from unpasteurized or raw milk (*lait cru* in French)—as opposed to pasteurized milk—is more flavorful.

The word "cheese" derives from the Middle English *chese*, Germanic *kasjus*, and Latin *caseus*.

# Classifying Cheese

Cheese can be grouped into as many as ten different categories. This table and key divide cheeses into basic types, with examples of each. They also provides information on how they're made, as well as their variety of milk, country of origin, and key characteristics.

**CHEESE BY TYPE** "Fresh" cheeses, such as feta, sheep's milk ricotta, and some goat's milk cheeses, are a bit too mild or loose for a cheese-tasting, therefore I have not included them in the table above.

**CHEESE BY MILK** Many cheeses are prepared with several types of milk (Juustoleipa, from Finland, is made from cow and reindeer milk). Some cheeses traditionally made with one milk type are now made with different types, like goat Camembert.

**CHEESE BY COUNTRY** In general, warmer regions produce softer, fresher cheeses, while colder regions make harder, longer-aged, and longer-lasting cheeses. Sheep and goat cheeses are usually made in drier areas, such as Provence, southern Italy, and much of Spain, while cow's milk cheeses come from verdant areas, like Switzerland and the United Kingdom.

**CHEESE BY CHARACTERISTICS** Some cheeses, such as Crottin de Chavignol, can be hard when long-aged and soft when barely aged.

## Classified CHEESE ☞ KEY ☜

**✳ SOFT-RIPENED OR BLOOMY RIND**
During aging, these cheeses are salted and exposed to mold, which forms a white "bloomy" rind. The cheese ripens from the outside in, resulting in a rich creamy interior.

**⊞ BLUE-VEINED**
Spores are added to the curd. Later, the cheeses are pierced to allow carbon dioxide to escape and oxygen to enter, encouraging growth of blue-green-purple mold. The resulting (unpressed) cheeses are strong in flavor.

**⊞ COOKED, PRESSED**
Curds are heated until they become solid, and then pressed. The cheeses are aged for up to 6 years, and often have holes, caused by gas expansion within the curd during ripening.

**✿ UNCOOKED, PRESSED**
Curds are heated to a lower temperature, then divided into small pieces and pressed. Aging takes at least 2 to 3 months, during which the rind is continually brushed to ensure a smooth, humid-free surface.

**※ GOAT**
Goat's milk curds are ladled into molds, resulting in a flaky texture. Goat cheese varies from soft, fresh, and a bit chalky to firm, aged, and somewhat crumbly.

**❀ SOFT, WASHED RIND**
During a 2- to 6-month aging, these strong-flavored cheeses are soaked, brushed, rubbed, or washed in brine, beer, wine, or grape brandy to encourage the growth of exterior mold.

| · TYPE · | · MILK · | · COUNTRY · | · CHARACTERISTICS · |
|---|---|---|---|
| �֎ Camembert de Normandie | Cow | France | Soft, creamy, buttery, earthy at times |
| �֎ Brie de Meaux | Cow | France | Soft, creamy, buttery, earthy at times |
| �֎ Explorateur (triple cream) | Cow | France | Soft, rich |
| ✖ Saint-Marcellin | Cow or Goat | France | Semi-soft |
| ⊞ Gorgonzola | Cow | Italy | Semi-soft, creamy |
| ⊞ Roquefort | Sheep | France | Soft, creamy, salty, strong |
| ⊞ Maytag Blue | Cow | USA | Soft |
| ⊞ Stilton | Cow | England | Semi-hard, buttery and crumbly, full-flavored |
| ⊞ Cabrales | Cow, Sheep, and Goat | Spain | Semi-soft |
| ⊞ Parmigiano-Reggiano | Cow | Italy | Hard, complex, sweet, nutty |
| ⊞ Gruyère | Cow | Switzerland and France | Semi-hard to hard, fruity, nutty |
| ⊞ Fontina d'Aosta | Cow | Italy | Semi-hard, nutty, fruity |
| ⊞ Comté | Cow | France | Semi-hard, similar to Emmentaler (Swiss) cheese, fruity |
| ⊞ Beaufort | Cow | France | Semi-hard, fruity, similar to Emmentaler |
| ✺ Saint Nectaire | Cow | France | Semi-soft |
| ✺ Morbier | Cow | France | Semi-hard |
| ✺ Manchego | Sheep | Spain | Hard, sweet to nutty |
| ✺ Cheddar | Cow | England | Hard, deepens in flavor as ages |
| ✺ Lancashire | Cow | England | Semi-hard |
| ✺ Pecorino | Sheep | Italy | Hard |
| ✺ Reblochon | Cow | France | Soft |
| ✺ Gouda | Cow | Netherlands | Hard, mild when young and nutty, complex, and redolent of caramel when aged (known as *Boerenkaas*) |
| ✳ Selles-sur-Cher | Goat | France | Soft |
| ✳ Valençay | Goat | France | Soft |
| ✳ Crottin de Chavignol | Goat | France | Soft to hard (depending on age), becomes spicy and nutty as it ages |
| ✾ Époisses de Bourgogne | Cow | France | Soft, oozing, rich |
| ✾ Livarot | Cow | France | Semi-soft, very smelly, meaty, nutty |
| ✾ Muenster | Cow | France | Soft, nutty, strong |
| ✾ Taleggio | Cow | Italy | Semi-soft to soft, strong, beefy |
| ✾ Vacherin du Haut-Doubs | Cow | France | Soft |

# FIND YOUR
# CHEESE

When tasting cheeses, go for a variety of samples. That way, you'll relish and discover new cheeses, while avoiding monotony. This is especially recommended for novices, where everyone will want to get a sense of the different types of cheese.

Try six cheeses, among them mild, strong, soft, and hard varieties. Mix up the types of milk: include sheep's, goat's, and cow's milk samples. Feature young cheeses and harder, long-aged varieties. Experience some from France, others from Italy, and still others from Spain. Purchase a few rounds, a pyramid, and a couple of rectangular cheeses. Include a washed rind cheese (where the rind is reddish or orange in color), a pure white cheese, and a goat cheese that's been covered in black ash.

All that said, it's fun to taste cheeses from only one country, such as France. The country produces such a wide variety of cheeses, your tasting will be anything but monotonous!

Whatever you choose, try to include the highest-quality products you can find (see the sample Menus on pages 82–83).

## SHOPPING FOR CHEESE

Shopping for cheese is much more difficult than shopping for packaged, long-shelf-life items, like olive oil, honey, or chocolate. Cheese is a living, breathing thing, whose storage and care are essential to maintaining quality. As a result, if possible, try to purchase cheese from trusted, reputable cheesemongers with high turnover. You want to be sure the merchandise

is moving, as you can't always tell how long it's been in the bin (of course, always check the sell-by date). You might want to ask your cheesemonger how he or she stores cheese; it should be kept in a humid environment of 50–60°F. The wrapping on cheeses should also be changed frequently, and some cheeses should even be misted to prevent them from drying out. (Note: These storage rules are for aged cheeses, rather than fresh, which should generally be kept at cooler temperatures.)

Avoid cheeses with a highly unpleasant odor, including those that smell and taste of ammonia. Other warning signs include: wet, sticky packages and excessive sliminess; paste (interior of the cheese) that's pink in color or shrunken in the rind; and dry, cracked edges. Also, look for natural rinds, as opposed to wax or plastic, the latter being signs of large-scale factory production.

If you can, purchase cheese cut fresh from the log or wheel. Cheeses require oxygen, and shrink-wrapping makes it more likely that they'll take on undesirable odors and flavors.

It's also important to be aware that cheese names can be deceiving. For example, the cheese aisles in U.S. grocery stores often include a bevy of Brie and Camembert; however, these products are not the "real thing." True Brie and Camembert are called Brie de Meaux au lait cru (raw milk) and Camembert de Normandie au lait cru. Made from raw milk, they are aged for less than 60 days, and, as a result, are not allowed into the United States. Versions you'll see in the States are, thus, made from pasteurized milk or are aged longer than 60 days. Sometimes these cheeses approximate the flavor and texture of "the real thing," but often, they're just pale imitations.

To make sure that you're buying what you think you're buying (namely, "authentic" cheeses), look for the French AOC, Italian DOC, Portuguese DOC, or Spanish DO on the label, as well as the full name of the cheese (for example, "Tomme de Savoie," not just "Tomme"). These designations ensure that the product is "protected," that is, made using a specific type of milk and means of production, most likely carried out for hundreds of years.

At the cheese shop, read any descriptions of the cheeses and ask the cheesemonger which products are recommended. Which cheeses are at the perfect stage of ripeness? Which are farmhouse? Which are raw milk? Do they have any unusual cheeses? Most importantly, try to taste everything.

Given the importance of pre-tasting and inspecting cheese, I'm a bit wary of purchasing cheese over the Internet; however, there are a number of excellent vendors online. Some even offer cheese accompaniments (such as quince paste), as well as cheese courses, making the selection of samples that much easier. Try www.artisanalcheese.com, www.formaggiokitchen.com, www.murrayscheese.com, or www.zingermans.com.

# STORING CHEESE

Since most of us don't have access to cheese caves, it's a good idea to just buy the amount of cheese that you'll be serving and to consume it within a few days. If you can, make your purchases the day of your tasting (or the day before) for the freshest product.

Leftover cheeses can be wrapped in papers (such as parchment) so that they can breathe. Make sure to wrap hard cheeses, such as Parmigiano-Reggiano, adequately, since they have a marked tendency to dry out. Blues should be wrapped in foil. Murray's Cheese Shop in Manhattan advises storing fresh cheeses (such as feta) in airtight containers, and moist and crumbly cheeses (like Caerphilly) in a slightly dampened cloth.

Store your cheeses as close to the bottom of the fridge as possible, preferably in the vegetable drawers, which should be fairly humid.

In terms of keeping times, soft-ripened cheeses, such as Brie, should last for at least a week. Hard cheeses should keep for several months.

If cheese molds, cut off about a ½-inch from the moldy sides and consume the rest within the week.

# CHOOSE YOUR
## ACCOMPANIMENTS

Nothing is more sensual and pleasing than experiencing superlative cheeses with wine, fruit, nuts, bread, and condiments. When purchasing your accompaniments, just follow the formula below:

FRUIT PRODUCTS One to two fresh varieties (such as champagne grapes, strawberries, figs, apples, pears, berries) and one to two dried (such as apricots or mango) or preserves/confits/chutneys (such as caramelized strawberries, fig preserves, mango chutney, candied citrus peel, or fig logs).

NUT PRODUCTS Plain (toasted almonds, pecans, walnuts), flavored (spiced, candied, or caramelized nuts; nut brittle; almonds in rosemary honey), or both.

BREAD PRODUCTS A baguette, nut bread, and possibly crackers.

MEAT PRODUCTS One or more cured meats, such as saucisson sec, proscuitto, or Serrano ham.

CONDIMENTS One or more condiments, such as honey, Port or balsamic reductions (see recipes on pages 60 or 85), or aged balsamic vinegar.

WINE You can serve a different drink with each cheese, or, keep things simple by offering only one of the following: sparkling wine, Riesling, Sauvignon Blanc, Pinot Noir, Côtes du Rhône, Zinfandel, or dessert wine.

# MENU

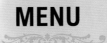

VARIED CHEESE TASTING
(EVENING)

## APPETIZER

CHAMPAGNE  *Blanc de Blancs, Brut*

TWO-PEPPER SHARP CHEDDAR GOUGÉRES

## TASTING

CHAMPAGNE  *Blanc de Blancs, Brut*

TOMME FLEUR VERTE  *France, goat's milk, herb-rubbed, fresh*

VACHERIN DU HAUTE JURA  *France, cow's milk, soft-washed rind*

CÔTES DU RHÔNE

KEEN'S FARMHOUSE CHEDDAR  *England, cow's milk, hard,
uncooked and pressed*

PECORINO TOSCANO DOC  *Italy, sheep's milk, hard, uncooked and pressed*

PETIT MUENSTER GÉROMÉ, JEAN ROUSSEY FROMAGE  *France,
cow's milk, soft-washed rind*

TAWNY PORT

COLSTON BASSETT STILTON  *England, blue-veined, cow's milk*

## ACCOMPANIMENTS

*Pears, strawberries, fig preserves, balsamic reduction, saucisson sec,
caramelized walnuts, baguettes, rosemary and fennel crackers*

# MENU

## APPETIZER

CHAMPAGNE *Brut*

RADISHES WITH BUTTER AND SEA SALT

WILD MUSHROOM QUICHE WEDGES

## TASTING

SANCERRE OR SAUVIGNON BLANC

SELLES-SUR-CHER *goat's milk, soft-ripened*

CHARDONNAY *(such as White Burgundy)*

CHAOURCE *cow's milk, bloomy rind, unpressed
and uncooked*

BANON *cow's, sheep's, and goat's milk, unpressed and uncooked,
wrapped in chestnut leaves*

BEAUFORT (RAW) *cow's milk, cooked*

SAUTERNES

ÉPOISSES *cow's milk, washed-rind, uncooked, unpressed*

ROQUEFORT (RAW) *sheep's milk, blue-veined*

## ACCOMPANIMENTS

*Champagne grapes, caramelized strawberry preserves, saucisson sec,
toasted almonds, baguettes, nut bread*

## RECIPES FOR ACCOMPANIMENTS

There's no real need to cook when having a cheese tasting, but if you're so inclined, feel free to whip up these simple, quick preparations. The balsamic reduction and caramelized nuts are delicious partners for almost all cheeses, but especially Parmigiano-Reggiano, hard sheep's milk cheeses, and blue cheese varieties.

### TWO-PEPPER SHARP CHEDDAR GOUGÈRES

(MAKES ABOUT 48)

*The gougères, best served warm, can be refrigerated for 2 days or frozen for 1 week. Reheat them by baking in a preheated 350° F oven for 10 minutes (if previously refrigerated), or 15 minutes (if frozen). Adapted from the "Mini Gougères" recipe published in the February 1996 issue of* Gourmet *magazine.*

- **1.** Preheat the oven to 375° F. Line two baking sheets with parchment paper. Place water, butter, salt, and sugar in a heavy medium saucepan. Bring to a boil. Turn off the heat and add the flour all at once. Stir until the dough becomes shiny and smooth, and forms a ball, about 3 minutes. Let cool for two minutes.

- **2.** Transfer dough to an electric mixer. Turn onto high speed and begin adding the eggs one at a time, beating well after each addition. (The batter should be shiny and fall off of the spoon a bit. If not, beat another egg in a small bowl, gradually add to the mixture, and beat with the electric mixer.)

- **3.** Beat in the Cheddar, cayenne, and thyme. Load the dough into a pastry bag or large freezer bag. If a freezer bag, once the dough is loaded, snip off a quarter-inch of one of the bottom corners. Using the filled bag, pipe the mixture into 1-inch-diameter circles (each about 1 tablespoon) on the parchment, spaced about 1 inch apart. (If you prefer, you can use a spoon to shape the dough.) Sprinkle with the Parmigiano-Reggiano and black pepper.

- **4.** Transfer one baking sheet to the middle rack of the oven and bake for about 30 minutes, until the tops are golden brown and the sides are somewhat firm and crisp. Repeat with the other batch. Let cool.

I cup water

I stick unsalted butter, cut into small pieces

½ teaspoon table or iodized salt

¼ teaspoon granulated sugar

I cup all-purpose flour

4 large eggs (note: sometimes 5 will be necessary)

1½ cups coarsely grated sharp Cheddar cheese

¼ teaspoon ground cayenne

½ teaspoon dried thyme leaves

⅓ cup coarsely grated Parmigiano-Reggiano cheese

Freshly ground black pepper to taste

## ADDICTIVE CARAMELIZED NUTS

(MAKES 1½ CUPS)

*Serve these nuts with salty cheeses, such as blue, or nutty cheeses, such as aged Gouda. You can prepare them up to one week in advance (store in a tightly sealed container).*

**•1•** Place granulated sugar in a medium-sized bowl and set aside. Add butter to a medium-sized nonstick skillet. Melt over low heat, about 1–2 minutes. Add walnut halves, and toast for about 2–3 minutes, until fragrant and coated with the butter. Add salt and dark brown sugar, and raise heat to low-medium (if the sugar is in clumps, break up with a wooden spoon).

**•2•** Cook for 3–4 minutes, stirring frequently: you want to make sure that all of the sugar melts and evenly coats the nuts (watch carefully, to ensure that the sugar doesn't burn). Remove the pan from the heat and immediately pour the nuts into the bowl of sugar. Stir until well coated. Cool and serve.

3 tablespoons granulated (white) sugar

2 tablespoons unsalted butter

1½ cups unsalted walnut halves

½ teaspoon Kosher or coarse salt

3 tablespoons (packed) dark brown sugar

## BALSAMIC REDUCTION

(MAKES ABOUT 1/3 CUP)

*Drizzle this over Parmigiano-Reggiano or Pecorino. Use an inexpensive balsamic vinegar; by cooking it down, you're concentrating its flavors to simulate the effect of an aged balsamic. Feel free to make this up to 1 week in advance (store in a tightly sealed container). See also the Port Reduction recipe on page 60.*

**•1•** Pour 1 cup of balsamic vinegar into a small, heavy saucepan. Bring to a boil over high heat, then reduce to a simmer over medium-low heat. Keep watching the pot, as the balsamic can burn. Simmer 8–10 minutes (less if you prefer a thinner reduction, more if you prefer a syrup).

# ORGANIZE YOUR
# TASTING

On the day of the tasting, remove the cheeses from the refrigerator one hour before the event, in order to give them a chance to
warm up to room temperature. (The cold dims flavors and gets
in the way of cheese's soft, sometimes melting texture.) Arrange
the cheeses on platters, marble or granite slabs, wooden boards,
or trays (leaving a few inches between them). Make sure to label
each cheese, either with a porcelain cheese marker or a folded
index card.

## What You'll Need

Before the tasting, make sure to have on hand "The Basics"
(see Chapter 1), as well as the materials at right.

Arrange the knives next to the
cheeses. Sharp steak or chef's knives
are fine—there's no need for fancy
cheese planes or specialized cheese
slicers. Just make sure the knives are
the appropriate sizes for the cheese
samples. Feel free to use the same
knife for all of your hard cheeses or
for different cheeses within the same
category (e.g., fresh goat, washed
rind, or soft bloomy rind); use a
clean cloth napkin to wipe the knives
between cheeses.

MATERIALS
Knives

Cloth napkins
(for wiping the
knives between
different cheeses)

A bucket
for excess wine

Appropriate
cheeses and
accompaniments

During the tasting, make sure to cut the cheese in such a way that each sample has some rind and some paste (interior). Also, cut smaller pieces of the heavier cheeses, such as Cheddar, as to not overwhelm. Exactly how you cut the cheese isn't too important though, generally, rounds are cut into wedges while slabs or logs are cut into thin slices (Cheddar and Parmigiano-Reggiano into small chunks).

## ACCOMPANYING DRINKS

Cheese can be served with many beverages, including wine (regular or fortified, such as Port and Sherry), pear or apple cider (alcoholic or non-alcoholic), fruit juice (such as white pear or grape, but not overly acidic citrus), beer, and fruit brandy, among others. Since the options can be overwhelming, I have provided some tips for wine—the most common beverage pairing—below:

> " A dinner that ends without cheese is like a beautiful woman with only one eye.
>
> —Jean-Anthelme Brillat-Savarin (Lawyer, politician, and author of *Physiologie du Goût,* 1755–1826) "

- Since you're having a cheese tasting—not a wine tasting—begin by purchasing the cheese. Then, ask the staff at your wine shop to recommend complementary wines within your budget.
- Although your cheesemonger might tell you to serve your cheeses in a certain order (from milder, simpler, younger, and lighter to stronger, more complex, aged, and heavy), this might not always be possible. Why? Wines, as well as cheeses, need to be served in a certain order—they should progress from light, dry, and white to heavy, sweet, and red. Once you've had a glass of the latter, you shouldn't return to the former. For this reason, you might need to adjust the order in which you'll try the cheeses around the order in which you'll need to drink the wines.

- Since cheese is the focus, don't drown it out by serving overly complex wines—save your expensive bottles for meals or for enjoying on their own.

- Either pair "like with like," or shoot for contrast. For example, serve a young goat cheese with a young, crisp white. Or, contrast salty, rich Gorgonzola with sweet sherry, syrupy Sauternes, or gourmet grape juice (such as the Pinot Noir variety from Navarro Vineyards). The same goes for fizzy, acidic Champagne and rich, creamy Pierre-Robert.

- Dry, tannic reds are difficult to pair with cheese; if you're craving a red, go for a fruity, slightly lighter variety (such as Beaujolais or Pinot Noir). For the most part, you'll want to avoid pairing red wines with blue cheeses, as the resulting taste is often metallic. White wines, such as Gewürztraminer, Pinot Gris/Grigio, Fumé Sauvignon Blanc, and Riesling, match well with many cheeses.

- Consider staying within countries or regions; for example, pair a Manchego with a Rioja; a French goat cheese, such as a Crottin, with a Sancerre; a Camembert with pear cider; and a California goat cheese with Sauvignon Blanc.

- Drink whites and sparkling wine at 45–50°F and reds at 60–65°F. Fortified wines should be served at room temperature.

- There's no need to rinse out wine glasses in between servings. In fact, any residual water can compromise the wine's flavor. By going from white to red and light to heavy wines, the flavors will not be muddled.

# LEARN YOUR
# PALATE

Whether you eat the rind during your cheese tasting is up to you. Try a small bite, and see if you like it. There's a good chance you won't with washed-rind cheeses, whose rinds are often gritty and bitter. Don't bother trying the very hard rind of hard, aged cheeses, such as Parmigiano-Reggiano, and, obviously, you'll want to refrain from munching on any wax, foil, or cloth rinds.

- **·1·** Study the cheese. What does it look like? Describe its color and shape.

- **·2·** Now, break off a very small piece of the cheese and rub it between your fingers. Place it in front of your nose (don't worry, you'll be enjoying the rest of it later). Inhale. What aromas do you detect?

- **·3·** Now, place the small piece of cheese on your tongue. Bite down and press it to the roof of your mouth. Circulate it, engaging all your taste buds. What flavor notes do you detect? What is the texture?

- **·4·** Swallow the cheese. Is the finish (or aftertaste) long or short, meaning do the flavors dissipate quickly or last for a while in your mouth? What flavors remain?

- **·5·** Do you like it?

# TASTING GRID

As you taste each cheese, write your answers to the questions on the previous page on a copy of this grid. Feel free to use the examples of tasting terms given below, and keep a record of the grid for future purchases.

| | •1• | •2• | •3• | •4• | •5• | •6• |
|---|---|---|---|---|---|---|
| **CHEESE NAME** | | | | | | |
| **APPEARANCE**<br>*Color and shape of the cheese. Appearance of rind: velvety, waxed, hard, soft, oiled.* | | | | | | |
| **AROMA**<br>*Ammoniated, herbal, tart, sweet, nutty, bland, strong, pungent, peppery.* | | | | | | |
| **FLAVOR**<br>*Earthy, rich, buttery, sharp, caramel, salty, nutty, milky, sweet, peppery, herbal, sour, tart, pungent, ammoniated, haylike, grassy, smoky.* | | | | | | |
| **TEXTURE**<br>*Soft, oozing, velvety, rubbery, hard, semi-soft, soft, creamy, semi-hard, smooth, firm, granular.* | | | | | | |
| **FINISH/DO YOU LIKE IT?**<br>*Long or short; which flavors remain?* | | | | | | |

# CHEESE
## *glossary*

**Affineur:** One who ages or ripens cheese (affinage refers to this process).

**Bloom:** The edible white rind of certain soft-ripened cheeses, such as Brie; formed by spraying the cheese surface with spores of *Penicillium candidum* mold.

**Chèvre:** French for goat, also refers to goat cheese.

**Coagulation:** The consolidation or curdling of milk solids.

**Curds:** Coagulated milk solids, the foundation of cheese.

**Farmstand/Fermière/Farmhouse:** Cheeses made on the same farm from which the milk was sourced; usually produced in an artisanal fashion.

**Mold:** Grows naturally on some cheeses; encouraged to grow in blue cheeses and on soft, bloomy-rind varieties.

**Paste:** The interior of the cheese, almost always softer than the rind.

**Pasteurization:** Heating milk above a certain temperature with the purpose of killing bacteria; this process is said to reduce the flavor of milk and, accordingly, of all cheese.

**Raw Milk (Lait Cru):** Unpasteurized milk.

**Rennet:** An enzyme added to milk to aid in the coagulation process; usually taken from the stomach of a calf, though vegetarian alternatives are available.

**Rind:** The exterior of most cheeses; some cheeses, such as ricotta salata or mozzarella, do not have a rind.

**Whey:** Liquid portion of milk.

# HONEY

*chapter five*

Glossy and sweet, honey seduces both children and adults alike. Anointed with just a drizzle of this "nectar of the gods," buttered toast is transformed into the most heavenly breakfast. When swirled with honey, plain yogurt is elevated to dessert, while hot honeyed tea pleases the palate, soothes the throat, and comforts the soul.

For centuries, this edible gold has been working its magic. Paintings from ancient Egypt illustrating beekeeping demonstrate that our ancestors knew a good thing when they saw it. Since then, honey has been put to myriad uses: as an offering to the gods, preserving bodies, healing wounds, and, of course, sweetening cakes. How about adding a modern-day honey tasting to the mix?

# KNOW YOUR
# HONEY

Honey is the only insect-made product we consume—and the only sweetener intact in its natural form (it takes a lot of processing to transform sugar cane or beets into sugar).

The story of honey begins with the humble honeybee, a type of bee that lives in a complex, hierarchical society, complete with its own division of labor. Each colony of bees features a queen, drones (male), workers (female), and infants in various stages of development. The queen bee is the mother of the hive, producing up to 3,000 eggs a day; the drones are the fathers—their one function is to mate with the queen. The workers maintain the hive, care for the infants, forage for nectar and pollen, and produce honey, which serves as food for the bees. (A mixture of nectar and pollen, called *beebread*, feeds the infants.)

Thirty- to sixty-thousand bees reside together in a single hive, the modern version of which is called a removable tray hive. These hives are often compared to filing cabinets, complete with stacked boxes, known as "supers." Each super holds eight to ten trays, onto which the bees secrete wax, forming the cells used to store pollen and honey (bees also secrete royal jelly, which feeds the queen and is used in some cosmetic products).

All honey is made from nectar, a sugary liquid produced by flowers. Every day, during the warm months, the worker bees take about ten trips, visiting blossoms and collecting nectar and pollen (a sticky protein). The bees store the nectar in an organ known as a *honey stomach* or *honey sac,* and the pollen on the hairs of their legs. During their journeys, bees transfer pollen from one flower's *stigmas* (male parts) to another's *ovules* (female parts), thereby pollinating them. In conducting this cross-pollination, bees ensure the continuation of various plant species. In some countries, as much as 80% of insect-crop pollination is done by honeybees.

After each run, the worker bees fly back to the hive, where they pass off the nectar they collected to other bees. These bees inject it with enzymes and fan it with their wings to evaporate much of its water content. Once this process is complete, the bees deposit the enriched and concentrated nectar into cells in the honeycomb and cap it with wax. The resulting honey is a mixture of sugar (about 70%, primarily fructose and glucose), water (roughly 17%), vitamins, minerals, and amino acids.

## ENTER THE BEEKEEPER

One honeybee will produce only $\frac{1}{12}$ teaspoon of honey in its entire lifetime.

During harvesting, the beekeeper exposes the hive to smoke, relaxing the bees. He or she then removes the trays with the honey and begins the extraction process. (Since the beekeeper provides a ready-made hive, the bees don't have to act as home construction workers and, thus, have more time to collect nectar and produce honey. This results in a surfeit of the sweet stuff, which the bees ostensibly don't mind our stealing.)

## HONEY IN ALL ITS FORMS

Honey is sometimes sold on the wax honeycomb (which has a pleasing chewy consistency). Otherwise, to remove it, beekeepers will usually warm the comb and scrape off the wax covering its cells. Next, most beekeepers spin the comb, centrifugally extracting the rest of the honey.

At this point, some honey is *pasteurized*, or heated to high temperatures to delay crystallization and to kill yeasts that can cause fermentation. The honey is then strained (to remove unwanted wax particles) and filtered (to purge any leftover pollen and air bubbles). Honey that is not heated, filtered, or blended is called "raw" or "unrefined."

Most honey is sold in liquid form. However, some honeymakers produce jars that are lighter in color and easier to spread. To make these "whipped" honeys (also called "creamed" or "churned"), the beekeeper adds "seed" honey crystals to liquid honey; as the crystals germinate and spread, they granulate the liquid honey.

In general, large manufacturers purchase honey from many beekeepers (sometimes from several countries) and then blend it to create a product that looks and tastes the same each year. These producers almost always pasteurize the honey by heating it to about 160°F, a temperature that many believe kills the enzymes that give honey its flavor and character. After straining and filtering, this honey is extremely clear and takes a long time to crystallize. In contrast, smaller, artisanal producers will often raise bees and make and package their own honey. They'll heat it to much lower temperatures (usually between 120–140°F), and sometimes bypass filtering and straining.

## STORING HONEY

Thankfully, storing honey couldn't be easier, largely because it doesn't spoil. What you're guarding against is crystallization, a natural process during which glucose precipitates out of the super-saturated solution. When this happens—and it usually will, after a few weeks or months—place the jar in a pan with warm water (with the heat off) and stir the honey until it liquefies. Alternatively, microwave on medium power for one minute. In general, you should store honey in an airtight container in a dry area. Do not store in the refrigerator (which spurs crystallization).

### 300 BOTTLES OF HONEY ON THE WALL

A honey's color and flavor are determined by the types of plants the worker bees visited on their daily trips. For the most part, though, the resulting honey doesn't have the flavors we associate with the plant. For example, blueberry honey tastes nothing like blueberries.

Some honeys, such as wildflower, are produced from the nectar of a range of blossoms that flower at the same time. Single varietals, on the other hand, are made with nectar from predominantly one type of plant, such as the avocado tree—predominantly, as opposed to entirely, since it's nearly impossible to ensure that bees visit only one type of blossom. To control for predominance, beekeepers try to release their bees into areas filled mostly with one type of plant, at a time when its flowers are nearly the only ones in bloom. This is made possible by the fact that beekeepers relocate their hives throughout the year, especially in spring and summer, to coincide with the blossoming of various plants.

It's worth pointing out that honey made from the nectar of the same type of plant, but grown in different places, such as Italy and California, will not taste exactly the same. This is because the plants themselves vary in character, due to differences in soil, water, and sunlight.

## A Few Honey Varieties

The varieties of honey can seem endless; the United States alone produces more than 300, of which clover is the most popular. The chart on the next page lists just a few types. Note that, in general, darker honeys are more flavorful, while lighter honeys are more subtle in taste. Whereas certain honeys are runny or clear, others are thick, opaque, and crystalline (the higher the honey's glucose level, the more crystalline its texture). French lavender and lehua honey crystallize quickly, whereas tupelo, fireweed, acacia, and sage honey almost never harden.

## Classified HONEY KEY

☞     ☜

✳ WATER WHITE

◉ EXTRA WHITE

■ WHITE

▨ EXTRA LIGHT AMBER

▦ LIGHT AMBER

✺ AMBER

※ DARK AMBER

❋ VARIED

*Note: According to the Pfund color grader—used by the honey industry to measure the color of honey—honey hue ranges from water white to extra white to white to extra light amber to light amber to amber to, finally, dark amber. None of the honeys in this chart are extra white or white.*

| · VARIETY · | · FLAVOR · | · REGION/COUNTRY · |
|---|---|---|
| ❄ Basswood (Also called lime or linden) | Strong, minty | USA (Alabama, Texas, Michigan), southern Canada |
| ❄ Kiawe | Very sweet, a bit minty | Hawaii |
| ❄ Lavender | Delicate, floral | France, Spain, USA (California) |
| ❄ Lehua (Ohia) | Buttery, brown sugar | Hawaii |
| ❐ Acacia | Delicate | USA (California), Italy, Eastern Europe |
| ❐ Sunflower | A bit tangy, spicy, and floral with citrus notes | Germany |
| ▦ Blueberry | Full, fruity, slightly tart | USA (Michigan, New England), Canada |
| ▦ Firewood/Fireweed | Delicate, sweet; tea or grassy notes | Northern and Pacific USA, Canada |
| ▦ Lemon Blossom | Citrus | Spain |
| ▦ Sourwood | Mild, spicy, astringent | USA (Appalachian Mts., from Pennsylvania to Georgia) |
| ▦ Yellow Star Thistle (Star thistle from Michigan results in a different honey) | A bit grassy, spicy | USA (California) |
| ❋ Corbezzolo (arbuta, strawberry tree) | Strong, bitter | Italy (Sardinia) |
| ❋ Leatherwood | Licorice, tart | Tasmania |
| ※ Avocado | Molasses and brown sugar | USA (California, Florida) |
| ※ Buckwheat | Pungent, bitter, molasses, and malt | USA (Minnesota, New York, Ohio, Pennsylvania, Wisconsin, Virginia), eastern Canada |
| ※ Carob | Caramel and menthol | Italy (Sicily) |
| ※ Chestnut | Strong, a bit bitter and smoky | North America, Italy |
| ※ Fir (sapin in French) | Anise | France, Greece |
| ※ Manuka | Slightly bitter, licorice | New Zealand |
| ※ Pumpkin | Sweet, spicy | USA |
| ※ Rosemary | Slightly bitter | France, Spain |
| ※ Tulip Poplar | Moderate flavor | USA (New England, Michigan, Gulf states east of Mississippi) |
| ※ Wild Thyme | Slightly bitter, herbal, grassy | Greece, New Zealand, France, Spain |
| ❀ Alfalfa | Mild, beeswax | Canada and USA (Idaho, Colorado, Nevada) |
| ❀ Clover | Mild, sweet, flowery | USA, Canada, New Zealand |
| ❀ Eucalyptus | Varies greatly, tends to be strong and slightly medicinal | USA (California), Australia |
| ❀ Heather | Bittersweet, buttery | USA (Michigan, New Jersey, West Virginia), Scotland, Italy (Sardinia), France (Corsica) |
| ❀ Mixed Wildflower: actually, made with a blend of wildflowers | Floral and sweet | USA, Italy, Australia, France |
| ❀ Orange Blossom | Mild, fruity, floral, citrus | USA (Florida, California, Texas, Arizona), Italy, Spain, Mexico |
| ❀ Safflower | Mild | Western USA |
| ❀ Sage, especially Black Button | Delicate | Southwest USA |
| ❀ Saw Palmetto | Spicy | Southeast USA |
| ❀ Tupelo | Delicate, floral, herbal, fruity | USA (Georgia, Florida) |

# FIND YOUR
# HONEY

It's fun to try a broad array of honeys. If you like, stick with products local to your area. For example, if you live in California, include eucalyptus, orange blossom, acacia, avocado, black button sage, and yellow star thistle. Otherwise, opt for sheer variety, featuring everything from runny, light-colored acacia; to medium-bodied blueberry; to dark, mahogany-rich chestnut. Avoid trying all mild or strong honeys—if you do, your tasting will grow monotonous.

## Shopping for Honey

Finding good-quality honey is simple. Start with your local gourmet store, farm, or farmer's market. Or venture online: www.zingermans.com, www.adrianascaravan.com, www.chefshop.com, www.agferrari.com, www.formaggiokitchen.com, and www.oakvillegrocery.com have extensive selections.

Look for artisanal brands, which tend to have more flavor. Also seek out raw honey, thought by most experts to be more complex than pasteurized honey. Varietals can be more interesting than blends, though wildflower honey, made from a flower mix, is an exception.

If you see anything about grades (A through C), ignore it. Grades refer in large part to the degree of refinement and clarity. Remember: the best honeys are often the least refined. In fact, a large number of excellent European honeys are ungraded.

Avoid infused honeys, which can be flavored with extracts or steeped with other ingredients. If you find a "strawberry honey," read the label to make sure it is honey made with nectar from the strawberry plant, and not honey mixed with pureed fruit.

# CHOOSE YOUR
## ACCOMPANIMENTS

For an afternoon tasting, begin with tea sandwiches (see sandwich suggestions on page 127 of Chapter 6: Tea) and cups of hot tea—preferably a black variety, such as Darjeeling. With the honeys themselves, serve fresh fruit (such as figs, apples, and pears), and cheeses (like goat, Manchego, Pecorino, or a young Cheddar). You can also set out a bowl or two of toasted nuts, such as pine nuts, hazelnuts, and walnuts.

Even though the honey is in itself a dessert, for an over-the-top event, offer a few sweets featuring the ingredient. Try honey cake, baklava, or other Middle Eastern pastries with a honey syrup. Otherwise, keep it simple, and bring out some vanilla ice cream; you can drizzle your favorite honey over it. Here's an even more novel idea: serve some mead, or honey wine.

## Shortbread Afternoon

To go with the afternoon tea theme, you could also prepare White Sesame Ginger Shortbread Cookies. In the shortbread cookie recipe in Chapter 6: Tea (see page 131), just substitute 2 teaspoons ground ginger for the matcha and cardamom, and use ¼ teaspoon, rather than ½ teaspoon, of salt. Add ⅓ cup finely chopped crystallized ginger along with the almond extract. In step 3, before placing the cookies into the oven, sprinkle with 2 tablespoons white sesame seeds. Skip the granulated sugar and Step 4 altogether.

# MENU

## APPETIZER

**DARJEELING TEA**

**ASSORTED TEA SANDWICHES**

## TASTING

**KIAWE** *Unheated and unfiltered organic white honey from Hawaii's Big Island, harvested after nectar is ripened by bees, but before honey crystallizes on the comb*

**LAVENDER** *Unheated, from Provence*

**TUPELO** *From northern Florida*

**BLUEBERRY** *From the United States*

**MANUKA** *From New Zealand*

**BUCKWHEAT** *From the United States*

## ACCOMPANIMENTS

*Baguette slices, fresh fruit, aged goat cheese, and toasted walnuts*

## Recipe for Afterwards

Honey can be used for far more than sweetening in cooking—it can also add its own unique flavors. Try drizzling honey over soft, fresh cheeses (such as ricotta, goat, and feta), yogurt, ice cream, crème fraîche, fresh fruit, and toast. One of my favorite snacks is fresh figs and Parmigiano-Reggiano cheese with acacia honey, or Greek yogurt topped with thyme honey and chopped toasted walnuts. You can also mix honey into softened butter or oatmeal.

## BRIOCHE SLICES WITH WARMED STONE FRUITS, LAVENDER HONEY, AND FRESH LEMON RICOTTA

### (MAKES 4 SLICES)

*This simple-to-prepare dish, inspired by the flavors of Provence, France, can be served for brunch or dessert. If you don't have lavender honey, use another delicate variety, such as acacia, wildflower, or tupelo. During the colder months, substitute imported strawberries for the stone fruits. Adjust the sugar depending on the sweetness of the fruit.*

•1• In a small bowl, mix the ricotta and lemon zest. Set aside.

•2• In a medium-sized skillet, melt the butter over medium heat until bubbling. Add the fruit, honey, salt, and fresh thyme, and let simmer for about 4 minutes, until warm and soft.

•3• Divide brioche among four plates. Ladle fruit mixture over each piece of bread, then top with a scoop of the ricotta, and garnish with additional honey. Serve warm.

½ cup fresh sheep's milk ricotta cheese

1 teaspoon freshly grated lemon zest

1 tablespoon unsalted butter

2½ cups ripe peach, nectarine, or plum slices (or hulled, halved strawberries)

3 tablespoons lavender honey, plus another teaspoon for garnish

Pinch coarse or Kosher salt to taste

1 teaspoon fresh thyme leaves

4 thick slices brioche, toasted

# ORGANIZE YOUR
# TASTING

In case you're tempted to bring out the booze, keep in mind that tasting honey and alcohol together may cloud your perception of the honey. To be on the safe side, stick with water.

## WHAT YOU'LL NEED

Before conducting the tasting, make sure to have on hand "The Basics" (see Chapter 1), as well as the materials below. If any of your honey is crystallized, place the jar(s) in warm water.

During the tasting, serve yourself with the spoon in each honey jar (you should take about a teaspoon of each variety). The honey should be drizzled onto a baguette slice or a cracker or two, as well as one of your (disposable) spoons. Used spoons can be discarded in the bucket.

Keep in mind that the brands of various honeys don't matter much, since honey is an entirely natural product. Furthermore, the degree of crystallization has no bearing on quality—the granularity of any given jar can vary dramatically, depending on age and storage.

### MATERIALS

Plastic spoons, 1 per taster per honey (place them beside each taster's plate)

Bucket or bowl (for used spoons)

Appropriate honeys (each with a serving spoon) and platters of accompaniments, including baguette slices or unsalted, mild white-flour crackers

# LEARN YOUR
# PALATE

Many of the terms in the tasting grid (on page 112) are taken from the National Honey Board (NHB). Some are not self-explanatory: The NHB defines medicinal as "like varnish, or the outer part of a mango," molasses prune as "like molasses, brown sugar, a caramelized flavor . . . prunes, or raisins," anise as "intensity of anise flavor like black licorice or anise candy," waxy as "intensity of waxy flavor like beeswax," spicy cinnamon "like Red Hot candies," and green "including any green growing thing or green unripened fruit." If these terms still don't resonate with you, feel free to come up with your own.

•1• Study the honey carefully. Describe its color, viscosity (flow), and level of clarity.

•2• Now, place your honey-filled spoon in front of your nose. Inhale. What aroma notes do you detect?

•3• Place the spoon in your mouth, spreading the honey all over your tongue. How would you describe its texture? What flavors are you experiencing?

•4• Next, swallow the honey. Is the finish (or aftertaste) long or short, meaning do the flavors dissipate quickly or last for a while in your mouth? What flavors remain?

•5• Consider whether you like the honey and would purchase it.

# HONEY TASTING GRID

As you taste each honey, answer the questions on the previous page and write your answers on a copy of this grid. Feel free to use the below examples of tasting terms, and keep the grid for future purchases.

| | ·1· | ·2· | ·3· | ·4· | ·5· | ·6· |
|---|---|---|---|---|---|---|
| **HONEY NAME** | | | | | | |
| **APPEARANCE** *Color; viscosity: high or low. Clarity: transparent or opaque.* | | | | | | |
| **AROMA** *Sweet, clover nectar, green, spicy cinnamon, waxy, flowery perfume, anise, molasses prune, sharp, lemon, medicinal.* | | | | | | |
| **TEXTURE** *Gritty, velvety, creamy, buttery, smooth, thick, thin, runny.* | | | | | | |
| **FLAVOR** *Sweet, nutty, green, spicy cinnamon, waxy, flowery perfume, anise, molasses prune, medicinal, fruity, barny, metallic, bitter, redolent of orange, caramel, molasses, mint.* | | | | | | |
| **AFTERTASTE** *Long or short. Sweet, flowery perfume, molasses prune, fruity, metallic, astringent.* | | | | | | |
| **DO YOU LIKE IT?** | | | | | | |

# HONEY

*glossary*

**Cold-Extracted:** Honey that is not warmed during extraction; thought to be more flavorful.

**Creamed (or Whipped):** Honeys to which honey granules have been added, spurring on crystallization and causing a lighter color, solid texture, and spreadable consistency.

**Crystallization or Granulation:** Solidification of honey; the greater the amount of glucose, the earlier this process begins.

**Filtered:** Honeys from which pollen and air bubbles have been removed.

**Nectar:** Sugary liquid produced by flowers; the basis of honey.

**Pasteurization:** Heating to high temperatures to kill yeasts and slow down crystallization; said to reduce the aroma and flavor of honey.

**Raw or Unrefined:** Honey that is not heated, filtered, or blended; thought to be more flavorful.

**Single Varietal:** Honey made with nectar from predominantly one type of plant.

**Strained:** Honey from which natural wax particles have been removed.

# TEA

*chapter six*

---

After water, tea is the most popular beverage in the world: While Buddhist monks sip their brew before meditating, denizens of the American South hydrate themselves with sweetened iced tea. In Japan, traditionalists conduct a ritual known as the tea ceremony (*chaji* or *chanoyu*), while in Morocco hosts pour mint-steeped green tea. At crowded train stations in India, it's difficult not to hear the tea-sellers advertising their milky, sugary wares; and, of course, who can resist British afternoon tea, with its black brews, buttery scones, clotted cream, and jam?

For something as simple as water steeped with dried leaves or buds, tea fulfills many purposes: it provides energy (in the form of caffeine), promotes healthfulness (with its polyphenols, which act as cancer-fighting antioxidants), and is a key part of religious and hospitality rituals.

According to legend, tea was discovered by the Chinese emperor Shen Nong in 2737 BC. After a few tea leaves dropped into his cup of boiling water, the emperor tried the infused beverage and was mightily impressed. Soon afterwards, tea became *the* drink in China, and later, the world.

# KNOW
# YOUR
# TEA

Although, by some accounts, over 15,000 types of tea exist, they all come from a single plant species: *Camellia sinensis*, an evergreen bush that thrives in subtropical and tropical climates. In addition to China and India (the largest tea grower), you can find tea gardens, estates, and plantations in Sri Lanka (referred to as *Ceylon* by the tea industry), Taiwan (called *Formosa*), Japan, Korea, Indonesia, Nepal, Australia, Argentina, and Kenya, among others.

Considering that all tea comes from one plant species, how can there be so many varieties? It all comes down to the three P's: provenance, picking, and processing.

## PROVENANCE

Put simply, provenance refers to where the tea leaves grew. With a few exceptions, teas cultivated at high altitudes (3,000–7,000 feet or more above sea level) are regarded as superior. Many experts feel that, since the leaves take a longer time to mature, they are more flavorful. As yields are lower and harvesting difficult, these teas are also more expensive than low-altitude varieties. Teas from prestigious regions, gardens, or plantations are considered premium as well.

## PICKING

One must also consider how and when picking occurred. Although, traditionally, tea is harvested by hand, it is now sometimes reaped by machine (generally in countries such as Japan, Taiwan, and Brazil, where labor costs make hand-picking prohibitively expensive). Even two teas picked in the same way can vary based on what exactly was picked. Although most tea is made from the smallest and youngest leaves and buds, it can consist of just the tip (bud), the tip and first two leaves, or the tip and three leaves, for example. With some exceptions, teas consisting of just buds, or buds and the first two leaves, are considered superior.

Timing also plays an important role: Leaves plucked during the first harvest of the season are known as *first flush*, while those picked in the second harvest are called *second flush*, and so forth. Although first flush teas are often hyped as being the best, it's truly a matter of personal preference; for example, some find first flush Darjeelings too delicate and subtle. To further clarify, John and Mike Harney of Harney & Sons offer the following observation: first flush is the greenest and most astringent, second is browner and very flavorful, and third (or autumnal) is brown and mellower.

## Processing

The final and most important determinant of a particular tea's traits is processing. Generally speaking, processing involves drying out tea leaves to prevent the growth of fungi, to develop flavor and color, and to produce a distinct appearance. Although processing methods vary, most teas are treated in the same basic fashion, though the order of the steps can differ significantly.

DRYING OR STEAMING After picking, black and oolong teas are dried out (withered) to reduce moisture and make the leaves softer and easier to work with (sometimes this process is hastened by circulating hot air underneath the leaves). Leaves for green, yellow, and white tea are steamed, or subjected to the rapid application of hot water. By destroying all enzymes, steaming preserves color.

SHAPING Once the leaves are withered or steamed, they are usually rolled into shapes to break up the leaf cells, releasing sap.

**OXIDATION** The oxidation process largely determines which category a tea falls into: white, green, yellow, oolong, or black. Sometimes called *fermentation* by the tea industry, oxidation involves exposing broken tea leaves—and their extracted sap—to air, thus allowing them to grow darker in color and to take on new aromas. White, yellow, and green teas are not oxidized and, hence, are sometimes referred to as *unfermented*. Generally, oolong teas are oxidized for about one to two hours and called *semi-fermented*, while black teas are oxidized for three to four hours, earning them the title *fermented*.

**FIRING** To halt the oxidation process, tea leaves are fired in an oven or over a fire. This causes additional moisture to evaporate and the sap to dry on the leaf, preserving the tea for shipment and sometimes adding flavor.

# GRADING TEA

After processing, some teas are graded by appearance: whole leaf, broken leaf, fannings (small pieces), or dust (tea in the last two categories often ends up in tea bags). The system for classifying black tea is considerably more byzantine, with almost 30 designations. Standard whole-leaf black teas are called "OP" ("Orange Pekoe"), while others fall into "FTGFOP1" ("Finest Tippy Golden Flowery Orange Pekoe First Grade Leaves"), "GFOP1" ("Golden Flowery Orange Pekoe First Grade Leaves"), and so forth. Since leaf characteristics don't always correlate to quality, you can pretty much ignore these designations; they're extremely confusing, even for tea aficionados.

All that being said, keep in mind that the exact processing of tea leaves varies from garden to garden, due to regional and personal preferences. Variation can even occur from batch to batch, since each group of leaves is distinct.

One relatively recent development in tea processing is the "CTC" method in which a large mechanical device uses metal rollers to cut, tear, and curl leaves. Since it forces more flavor out of tea leaves, this process can turn lower-quality raw materials into more saleable product (such as mass-market tea bags). For this reason, many experts regard machine CTC teas as inferior.

## Tea Varieties

The main types of tea are described in the chart at right. Within each of these categories are hundreds of varieties, named for the area in which they're grown, mythical figures, leaf appearance, and more. For example, Gunpowder green tea's rolled tea leaves resemble bullets. To make matters more complex, some teas, especially those produced in multiple countries, have many names.

Since tea leaves are a natural product with a great deal of variation, tea producers and packagers will often mix leaves from different crops to establish consistency (this is especially true of Ceylon teas). Tea producers may also combine different teas to create *blends*. For example, English Breakfast is traditionally a mixture of two or three types of black tea.

Packagers and importers may also flavor or scent teas, mixing in dried fruit, essential oils, or even spices. For example, in China and Taiwan, green tea is mixed with jasmine petals to form jasmine tea.

Herbal teas, like chamomile and peppermint, are not really teas at all, but rather *tisanes* or infusions, because they don't include tea leaves—just flowers, fruits, herbs, roots, seeds, or spices. Tisanes can be delicious, however, and, since they usually lack caffeine, are a good choice near bedtime.

*Classified*
# TEA
## KEY

**☀ BLACK**
Black teas account for most of the tea in the world and have the strongest flavor. Unblended black teas are named for where and when they grew, as well as the size of their leaves after processing.

**⊠ OOLONG**
The most costly of these varied "semi-fermented" teas hail from Taiwan (Formosa).

**▦ GREEN**
Generally, Chinese green teas are pan-fried, while Japanese green teas are steamed. Some experts describe Chinese green teas as golden-green in color; many have unusual leaf styles. Japanese green teas tend to be a brighter green, with a grassy, sea-like flavor.

**❀ WHITE**
White teas are produced from young leaves (or buds) that have been shielded from sunlight, preventing the formation of chlorophyll and a green color. Like green teas, they are not oxidized, and are often expensive, as they are produced in small quantities.

**※ BLENDED, SPICED, FLAVORED**
Often, tea leaves are mixed with pieces of dried fruit or spices, or perfumed with essences or oils, for flavored, scented, or spiced tea.

| · TYPE · | · FACTS · | · FLAVOR · | · COUNTRY · |
|---|---|---|---|
| ✳ Keemun | The base for many English Breakfast teas | Winy and chocolaty in flavor, slightly smoky | China |
| ✳ Darjeeling | The Tea Board of India uses a Darjeeling certification mark for authenticity | Medium-bodied, astringent, redolent of (Muscat) grapes, complex, long aftertaste | India |
| ✳ Ceylon | Consumed alone and in blends. The Dimbulla, Uva, and Nuwara Eliya districts produce premium leaves | Subtle, not astringent, though flavor can vary greatly | Sri Lanka |
| ✳ Assam | Assam is grown near sea level | Full, malty, with high tannin content | India |
| ✳ Lapsang Souchong | Withered and dried over smoky wood fires, this tea is produced strictly for export | Smoky, oaky, strong | China and Taiwan |
| ✳ Pu-erh | Known as "black" in China, where it originates, Pu-erh tea is most often compressed into bricks or cakes. Also available as "green" or "mature." | Strong, earthy | China |
| ⊞ Ti Kuan Yin (Iron Kuan Yin) | "Monkey-Picked" identifies superior varieties | Intense, fruity, flavorful | China |
| ⊞ Formosa (Taiwan) | Opt for Fancy, Fanciest, or Extra Choice grades | Redolent of ripe peaches | Taiwan |
| ⊞ Gunpowder | Most popular green tea in the Middle East ("Temple of Heaven Special Grade" is the premium variety) | Strong, flowery | China, Taiwan, and Sri Lanka |
| ⊞ Dragon Well | Most esteemed green tea in China | Hay-like, sweet, vegetal | China |
| ⊞ Sencha | Most popular tea in Japan | Grassy, tannic | Japan |
| ⊞ Gyokuro | Premium Japanese green tea | Vegetal, intense, a bit sweet | Japan |
| ⊞ Matcha | Ground Gyokuro tea whipped to a vibrant green froth; used in Japanese tea ceremony and in, green-tea ice cream | Thick, velvety, bitter | Japan |
| ❋ Bai Hao Yinzhen (Silver Needles) | At about $100 per pound, among the world's most expensive teas. | Pale, subtle, fresh | China |
| ❋ Ceylon Vintage Silver Tips | Includes only the whole terminal buds—no leaves | Light, sweet | Sri Lanka |
| ❋ Jasmine (scented) | Green or Pouchong tea (very lightly fermented tea, between Green and Oolong) leaves | Floral | China and Taiwan |
| ❋ English Breakfast (blended) | Usually consists of two or three black teas | Strong, rousing | England |
| ❋ Earl Grey (blended, scented) | Usually consists of two or three black teas, scented with bergamot oil | Strong, citrus-y | England |

# FIND
# YOUR
# TEA

For your first tea tasting, it's helpful to include different types of tea (see the menus on page 128–129). This way, you'll get to know the basic varieties.

Once you've had an introductory tasting, it's fun to move on to a tasting featuring only one type of tea. Since it can be monotonous to taste just one specific variety, such as Keemun, try sticking within a general category, like black or oolong. (Keep in mind that white and yellow teas are especially subtle, and might not appeal to a broad range of palates.)

In order to keep things interesting, aim for variety within the category you've chosen: teas with different-colored liquors (tea liquid), flavors, strengths, and provenances. For example, within the category of green teas, compare and contrast Chinese and Japanese varieties. Do you find that the Japanese varieties have a hint of sea flavor? Are they a brighter green color? If including all black teas, determine whether or not you prefer Darjeeling to Assam. Do you find the Darjeeling to be more delicate and complex in flavor?

Although tisanes and flavored teas are more than worth keeping on hand, you probably won't want to include them in a tea tasting since the former are not really tea, and the flavors in the latter can obscure the nature of the tea leaves. Likewise, despite their convenience and affordability for everyday use, I recommend sidestepping tea bags in favor of whole leaf teas for a tasting. The quality of tea bags is improving markedly (from packets of fannings of indeterminate origin to quality broken tea leaves);

however, whole leaf teas are typically more flavorful and beautiful, and offer a more authentic tea experience.

Six types of tea should make for a comprehensive, though not overwhelming, tasting. When selecting teas for your tasting, engage the services of your local tea shop, or read the product descriptions on various vendor Web sites. You can also consult the chart on page 121.

## SHOPPING FOR TEA

Since adulteration and false marketing afflict the tea industry, it's best to seek out reputable shops and Web sites, such as www.harney.com, www.inpursuitoftea.com, www.republicoftea.com, www.serendipitea.com, and www.adagio.com. For Japanese green tea, try www.japanesegreenteaonline.com or www.teastea.com. (Other Web sources include www.deandeluca.com, www.kyelateas.com, www.mightyleaf.com, and www.rishi-tea.com.)

If you can, try to taste teas before purchasing: even though a certain variety is famed or recommended by experts, it still may not please your palate. Feel free to ask for a taste in the shop.

# COLLECTING TEAWARE

Traditionally, different teas have been steeped in their own unique teapots. For example, oolongs are generally brewed in clay pots from Yixing, China, while Japanese green teas are steeped and served in small cast-iron pots.

If you're about to hit the store, keep in mind that unglazed ceramic teapots absorb aromas and flavors and, hence, should only be used for tea. By the same token, porcelain teapots with white interiors—perennially popular for preparing British-style tea—may stain with repeated exposure to dark teas.

Glass is a particularly practical and stylish option: it doesn't stain and allows you to watch the steeping process—especially beautiful when whole leaves are used (www.adagio.com offers a number of styles). Ideally, your tea cups should be made of glass, or feature white interiors, to reveal the color of the tea liquor.

When planning how much tea to buy, figure on ¼ cup of each sample per person. For a six-person tasting of six teas, purchase about one tablespoon of each type of loose tea. To be on the safe side, I would allot an extra tablespoon of each tea, just in case you decide to brew another pot or two at the end of the tasting (or find yourself craving tea the next day).

Whichever teas you purchase, make sure to immediately place the leaves into airtight containers—one for each variety—and store in a cool, dark, dry place. Tea loses its flavor over time, so try to drink it within a year.

## Trends in Tea

Tea has come a long way from instant tea and iced-tea mixes. Spurred on by publicity about its health benefits, tea—in particular, antioxidant-rich green tea—is now everywhere, from convenience stores to cosmetics counters. (Yes, some cleansing lotions and moisturizers are made with green tea.)

While *chai* (a sweetened drink of black tea, milk, and spices) has been the hot coffeehouse beverage for years, *bubble tea*, consisting of sweetened tea and tapioca balls, is manna to the young. Tea can even be found on restaurant dessert menus—have you ever tried green tea crème brûlée or earl grey tea chocolate cake?

With consumers becoming ever more tea-savvy, tea bags (which used to include low-quality tea dust) now consist of higher-quality leaves. Even more exciting: as of recently, iced tea comes in novel flavors, such as pomegranate white tea or rose green tea.

> " The best quality tea must have creases like the leather boots of Tartar horsemen, curl like the dewlap of a mighty bullock, unfold like a mist rising out of a ravine, gleam like a lake touched by a zephyr, and be wet and soft like a fine earth newly swept by rain. "
>
> — Lu Yu (Chinese sage, 733-804), *Cha Ching* ("The Classic of Tea")

# CHOOSE YOUR
## ACCOMPANIMENTS

Begin your tasting with a cup of tea—preferably the one you'll be tasting first. Try some tea sandwiches for a Continental-style tasting, or steamed *shumai* (Japanese dumplings, available at many grocery stores as well as Asian food shops) for a Japanese green-tea tasting.

Tea sandwiches can include cucumber, radish, and chive butter on rye bread (just mix minced chives, salt, and pepper into unsalted butter for the spread); smoked salmon and dill-red onion butter on white bread (mix minced red onion, finely chopped fresh dill, salt, and pepper into unsalted butter); sharp Cheddar, unsalted butter, and apple or pear butter on white bread; turkey and mango chutney on raisin-nut bread; egg salad with fresh dill and watercress on pumpernickel bread; and more.

Whatever type of sandwich you serve, make sure to remove the crusts. You can even form shapes with a cookie cutter. To prevent sogginess, spread butter on both interior sides of the bread; you can atone the next day!

When tasting the teas themselves, offer butter cookies, shortbread, biscuits, or scones for a Continental-style event. (Don't forget to serve jam and clotted cream or butter.) If making scones yourself, try the Fig and Orange Scones on page 130. For an Asian-themed tea, serve Asian-inflected shortbread (try the Almond Green Tea recipe on page 131), *wagashi* (artful Japanese sweets, usually prepared with fruits, nuts, seeds, and bean paste), *mochi* (sweet rice cakes), almond cookies, or steamed cakes. Visit your Asian grocery store; you'll surely find a trove of treats there.

# MENU

VARIED TEA TASTING

(AFTERNOON)

## APPETIZER

GUNPOWDER GREEN *Chinese*

ASSORTED TEA SANDWICHES *cucumber, radish, and chive butter; smoked salmon with dill-red onion butter; Cheddar and mango chutney*

## TASTING

GUNPOWDER GREEN *Chinese*

TI QUAN YIN—SPRING FLORAL *Chinese Oolong*

FORMOSA OOLONG *Taiwan*

TEMI SIKKIM *Darjeeling black*

KEEMUN MAO FENG *Chinese black*

MATCHA *Ground Japanese green*

## ACCOMPANIMENTS

*Port-Infused Fig and Orange Scones*

# MENU

## APPETIZER

SENCHA *Japanese, most popular tea in Japan*

STEAMED SHUMAI (JAPANESE DUMPLINGS)
WITH DIPPING SAUCE

## TASTING

SENCHA *Japanese, most popular tea in Japan*

GYOKURO-KARIGANE-CHA *Japanese, blend of two green teas, with leaves and stalks*

GENMAI-CHA *Japanese, blend of Sencha with roasted rice*

LUNG CHING OR DRAGON WELL *Chinese, with flat green leaves*

MATSUCHAIRI-SENCHA *Japanese, blend with Sencha*

YIN HAO JASMINE *Chinese, with green and black leaves, flavored with jasmine petals*

## ACCOMPANIMENTS

*Almond-Scented Green Tea Shortbread with Cardamom Sugar, wagashi*

# RECIPES FOR ACCOMPANIMENTS

If you're inclined to bake, try the following recipes. The scones are perfect for Continental-style teas, while the shortbread is delicious with all teas—especially Asian-style teas.

## PORT-INFUSED FIG AND ORANGE SCONES

MAKES ABOUT 24

*These scones can be prepared up to one week in advance (if stored in an airtight container). Alternatively, they can be frozen for up to one month and reheated in a 400° F oven for about 20 minutes. Nevertheless, they're best baked right before the tasting and served warm.*

•1• Preheat the oven to 350° F. In a small saucepan, bring the Port and figs to a boil. Remove from heat, cover, and let sit until cool, about 15 minutes. Drain very well, pushing down on the figs to remove all of the liquid. Set the liquid aside for another use (such as salad dressing). In a small bowl, place the drained figs, 2 teaspoons of orange zest, and ½ teaspoon of ground cinnamon, and combine well.

•2• In a large bowl, combine the remaining cinnamon, flour, sugar, baking powder, baking soda, and salt. Cut the butter into the flour. Crumble the mixture until a coarse meal forms. Stir in the fig mixture. In a medium bowl, combine the buttermilk and 2 well-beaten eggs. Stir into the flour and fig mixture.

•3• Form the dough into two balls and place on a flour-lined surface. Pat into two flat disks, each about 1 inch high. Then, cut each disk into 6 wedges. Cut each wedge in half, ending up with 24 wedges. Line two baking sheets with parchment paper and top with the wedges. In a small bowl, mix the 1 tablespoon of buttermilk with 1 egg. Using a pastry brush, apply to the tops of the scones. Sprinkle with the teaspoons of granulated raw sugar. Chill for about 10 minutes.

•4• Place the baking sheet on the upper and lower racks of the oven, and change their places after about 15 minutes. Bake until golden brown on top and a toothpick inserted into their centers comes out clean, 25–30 minutes total.

¾ cup Port wine

1⅓ cups finely diced dried black mission figs

2 teaspoons orange zest

1 teaspoon cinnamon, divided

4 cups all-purpose flour

6 tablespoons granulated sugar

2 teaspoons baking powder

2 teaspoons baking soda

¾ teaspoon salt

2 sticks chilled, unsalted butter, cut into pieces

1 cup plus 2 tablespoons chilled buttermilk, plus 1 additional tablespoon for the egg wash

3 large eggs, divided

2 tablespoons plus 1½ teaspoons granulated raw sugar

## ALMOND-SCENTED GREEN TEA SHORTBREAD
## WITH CARDAMOM SUGAR

MAKES ABOUT 24

*These flavorful and complex bright green cookies are not only delicious tea accompaniments—they actually contain tea! If you can't find* matcha, *just purchase another type of Japanese green tea, and grind it into a powder with a spice grinder. Technique adapted from* Bon Appetit Magazine, *March 1997.*

•1• In a medium bowl, mix the flour, sugar, *matcha*, cardamom, and salt until well-combined. Using an electric mixer, beat the butter on high speed until light, about 2 minutes. Add the extract and beat until combined. Beat the flour mixture into the butter mixture in four additions on low speed until well-combined.

•2• Transfer the dough to a flat surface and divide in half, forming each half into a 6-inch log. Then, form each log into a 2x1x6-inch-long rectangle. Cover in plastic and refrigerate for 2 hours.

•3• Preheat oven to 325°F. Grease two large baking sheets with butter. Remove dough from the refrigerator and cut into ½-inch-thick slices. Place slices on the baking sheets, making sure the cookies are at least 1 inch apart from each other. Transfer to the oven. After 10 minutes, switch the sheets so that the one on the bottom rack is now on the top (and vice versa). Bake until the cookies are lightly golden on the edges, about 25 minutes total. Let cool about 5 minutes.

•4• In a small bowl, mix the 3 tablespoons of granulated sugar with the ½ teaspoon of ground cardamom. One by one, carefully toss each cookie in the mixture, coating both sides in sugar. Let cool.

2 cups all-purpose flour

½ cup powdered or confectioner's sugar

1 tablespoon plus 1½ teaspoons *matcha* (powdered Gyokuro green tea)

1 teaspoon ground cardamom, plus a heaping ½ teaspoon for dusting

½ teaspoon salt

2 sticks unsalted butter, at room temperature, plus another 1 tablespoon for greasing baking sheets

1 teaspoon almond extract

3 tablespoons granulated sugar

# ORGANIZE YOUR
# TASTING

Arranging a tea tasting can be a bit complicated. You might want help keeping track of the amount of steaming water in the kettles and tea-steeping times. Create a cheat sheet for yourself with the name of each tea, the quantity of dry leaves and water you'll need, the recommended water temperature, and the steeping time (for a tasting for eight people, you'll probably prepare a total of two cups of each tea). Some tea merchants will automatically provide all of this information, but if not, just consult the package, as well as online merchants' Web sites. Place this cheat sheet next to the range as you prepare the teas.

## WHAT YOU'LL NEED

Before conducting the tasting, make sure to have on hand "The Basics" (see Chapter 1), as well as the materials listed at right. If you decide to serve *matcha* (see sidebar on page 135), you'll also need a whisk and a small or medium bowl to mix it in. If you are conducting a tasting involving black tea, you might want to have sugar, lemon, milk, and crystallized ginger to try with it. Also have on hand clotted cream or butter and jam for scones (see recipe on page 130).

MATERIALS
1 small tea/coffee
cup for everyone

1 medium-large
bowl/bucket for
pouring out excess tea

18 small bowls/ramekins

1 teapot with
an infuser/filter

2 kettles

Teaspoon measure

Graduated (liquid)
measuring cup

Timer

Appropriate teas and
accompaniments

## Set the Table and Organize the Tea

If you can, have your tasting in or near the kitchen—that way, you won't have to run back and forth with the teapot. Along the center of the tasting table, set down very small bowls (ideally matching), each filled with a different type of dried tea leaf (you will be evaluating their appearance). Since these leaves will later be discarded, use just a teaspoon. Label them with their names and with numbers, according to the order in which you'll try them—generally from mildest to strongest in flavor.

Next, line up the boxes of tea next to your range (and kettles) in the order in which you'll try them. On top of each box, place a small bowl, into which you've measured the appropriate amount of dry tea for brewing (probably 1 teaspoon per ¾ cup). In front of each box, place another small bowl. (You'll use this for the wet leaves, which can be brewed again.) Place the graduated measuring cup beside the tea boxes.

## Brew Tea For a Tasting

To prepare tea, do the following:

• 1 • Bring a kettle full of fresh, cold water to a boil. (For faster boiling, try an electric kettle, from a company such as Bodum or Braun.) When the water hits the boiling point, remove the kettle from the heat. (If you like, carefully rinse out your teapot and cups with the hot water.) For black or oolong teas, continue with the following steps. However, for green, yellow, or white teas, wait about five minutes before brewing the tea (for these types of tea, the water needs to come down a bit from the boiling point).

---

Afternoon tea was invented by an upper-class British lady (according to legend, Anna Maria, the seventh Duchess of Bedford of Woburn Abbey in Bedfordshire) to break up the time between lunch and dinner. High tea, often consisting of meat, cheese, and tea, was consumed by the British working class upon returning from the factory. Tea bags and iced tea were invented in the United States in 1904.

•2• Place the correct amount of loose tea in an infuser or very large tea ball (small tea balls don't allow teas room to breathe and spread out). While your tea vendor can provide specific guidance, you'll typically want to use one rounded teaspoon for every ¾ cup of water (and about twice as much for very mild varieties). Place the infuser or basket in the teapot. Measure the correct quantity of water in the graduated measuring cup and pour over the leaves.

•3• Cover the teapot and set the timer for the appropriate steeping time. Generally, you'll want to steep white teas for 30 seconds to 2 minutes, green teas for 30 seconds to 3 minutes, oolong teas for 3 to 5 minutes, and black teas for about 5 minutes. (Again, consult the package or your tea merchant for specific steeping times, as they can vary depending on the exact variety of tea.) Be sure to use a timer when preparing tea; if a pot steeps for too long, it becomes bitter; if it steeps for too short a time, it will be weak.

Note: If you decide to brew *matcha* (powdered Japanese green tea), pour 1 cup of hot (but not boiling) water over ½–1 teaspoon of tea (use more for a stronger brew). Vigorously whip the tea with a whisk (preferably bamboo; though stainless steel is fine) and serve.

•4• Meanwhile, keep the lid on the tea kettle—you'll be using the leftover hot water to prepare forthcoming cups of tea. Fill the second tea kettle with fresh, cold water. Bring this water to a boil. (Keep track of how much steaming water is in your kettles.)

•5• When the timer goes off, remove the infuser from the teapot and pour the wet leaves into the small bowl in front of the appropriate tea box (next to the range). Bring the teapot into the tasting area and place on the table. Pour the tea into each cup and taste. Repeat the process for all six teas, discarding excess tea (liquid) and rinsing out the teapot and infuser between each sample.

# LEARN YOUR
# PALATE

Try sugar, honey, lemon, milk, and crystallized ginger with black tea (if serving). However, taste it plain first. Also, make sure that you drink the tea while it's hot.

•1• Describe the appearance of the dry leaves. Are they whole or broken? Are the leaves twisted or flat, regular or uneven?

•2• Describe the color of the tea liquor (liquid).

•3• Close your eyes and inhale. What does it smell like?

•4• Now, slurp the tea—don't worry about making loud noises. Spread it all over your tongue and mouth. What flavor notes do you detect?

•5• Finally, swallow the tea. Is the finish (or aftertaste) long or short, meaning do the flavors dissipate quickly or last for a while in your mouth? What flavors remain?

•6• Most importantly, consider whether you like the tea and would purchase it.

# Tasting Grid

As you taste each tea, write your answers to the questions on the previous page on a copy of this grid. Feel free to use the tasting terms provided below, and keep this record for future purchases.

| | ·1· | ·2· | ·3· | ·4· | ·5· | ·6· |
|---|---|---|---|---|---|---|
| **TEA NAME** | | | | | | |
| **LEAF APPEARANCE** *Dry tea leaves: whole, broken, fannings (tiny pieces), dust (even smaller—literally like dust), twisted, flat, regular, uneven, rolled.* | | | | | | |
| **COLOR** *White, yellow, golden, yellow-green, light green, bright green, light brown, red, dark brown, black.* | | | | | | |
| **AROMA** *Floral, fruity, citrusy, smoky, strong, mild, malty.* | | | | | | |
| **FLAVOR** *Sweet, astringent, bitter, citrusy, peachy, floral, smoky, strong, delicate, complex, muscatel (reminiscent of the Muscat grape), malty, grassy, sea-like, vegetal, mild, subtle, bland, chocolaty, winey.* | | | | | | |
| **FINISH** *Long, short, what flavors remain?* | | | | | | |
| **DO YOU LIKE IT?** | | | | | | |

# TEA
## *glossary*

**Black:** Fully oxidized tea.

**Blended:** Two or more types of tea mixed together (e.g. Assam and Ceylon).

**CTC (Cut, Tear, Curl) Method:** A type of machine processing used for some black teas. Brings out flavors, allowing producers to use lower-quality tea leaves. CTC teas are often used for tea bags.

**Fannings or Dust:** Size-based grades, referring to very small pieces of tea leaf or literally tea dust; usually destined for tea bags.

**Flavored/Scented:** Tea leaves mixed with flavorings, such as oils, spices, dried fruits, or flower petals.

**Flush:** Harvest.

**Green:** Unoxidized tea.

**Liquor:** Tea liquid.

**Oolong:** Semi-oxidized tea.

**Orange Pekoe:** A size-based grade, referring to standard whole black tea leaves.

**Oxidation/Fermentation:** Exposure of tea leaves to air, bringing about the darkening of the leaves and the addition of flavors and aromas.

**Tisane (Herbal Tea):** A hot beverage made from herbs, roots, shoots, spices, or flowers. Not really tea since it doesn't contain any tea leaves.

**White:** Most delicate tea; unoxidized, with leaves shaded to prevent formation of chlorophyll.

**Whole Leaf:** Leaves still intact.

# EXTRA VIRGIN OLIVE OIL

*chapter seven*

According to ancient Greek mythology, the goddess Athena brought the first olive tree to the Greeks, and Zeus thanked her by naming the city of Athens in her honor. Olives are truly a gift from the heavens: Incredibly versatile, for thousands of years, their flesh and oil have been used for light, heat, food, and medicine.

As ancient as civilization itself—the fruits are thought to have first been cultivated in the Eastern Mediterranean as early as 6,000 years ago—olives are cherished throughout the Mediterranean, and now throughout the world. Today, they're even grown in China, Japan, Mexico, South America, South Africa, New Zealand, Australia, and the United States! This is a positive development for human health, since olive oil—especially extra virgin olive oil, which we'll be tasting—is brimming with cancer-fighting antioxidants and heart-healthy monounsaturated fat.

# KNOW YOUR
# OLIVE OIL

The olive is the fruit of the olive tree, or *Olea europaea,* an evergreen with gnarled branches and silvery green leaves. These fruits differ markedly depending on their variety, where and how they're grown, and the time and method of harvest. Although hundreds of varieties exist, two constants unite them: (1) Olives darken as they ripen, from light green to brown, purple, and then black. This means that a green olive could have come from the same tree as a black olive, but was just picked sooner. Green olives are flavorful, pungent, and crisp, with high levels of healthful polyphenols (antioxidants), whereas black olives are mild and sweet and soft in texture. The color of the oil is affected by many factors, including the soil, climate, type of olive, and time of harvest; however, generally, green olives produce green oil, while riper olives result in an oil that is more yellow in hue. (2) Olives are too bitter and tough to eat when picked, and must be either cured (to be consumed) in their original form, or pressed into olive oil.

## Extra Virgin Olive Oil: Fruit to Elixir

Good extra virgin olive oil begins with good-quality olives. In the fall or early winter, olives are picked by hand or machine. Most experts feel that hand-picking is superior to machine picking, since machines can bruise olives' skin, leading to rancidity.

After harvesting, the olives are taken to the mill, where they are washed and cleaned of leaves and branches. Next, they are pressed (ground or hammered into a paste using mechanically

driven stone wheels or rollers, metal-toothed grinders, or mechanical hammers). In order to prevent the flavor breakdown of the
olives, it's necessary to press them within 24 hours of picking at the
most. After pressing, the paste goes through the *malaxation* (or
mixing) process, during which the individual oil droplets coalesce
into larger drops (this makes the oil easier to separate later).

Oil juice and oil are separated from the *pomace* (fruit remains)
via a hydraulic press, centrifugal separator, or percolation. With the
first method (the most traditional), the paste is spread on stacks of
filters and then squeezed with a piston. Centrifugal separators spin
off the oil and water from the pomace. In percolation, metal discs
are continually dipped into the olive paste, and the oil is removed by
scrapers. Regardless of the method employed for the initial separa-
tion, oil is often further separated using a decanter.

Most just-pressed extra virgin olive oil
is allowed to settle for a few months before
bottling. If bottled without this holding period,
the product is known as *new oil, Aceite Nuevo,*
or *Olio Nuevo.*

Once they've settled, the oils may be
filtered or strained to remove any remaining
solids. Some artisanal producers, though, do
not filter their oil, resulting in a thicker product
(which is favored by some experts).

New or aged, unfiltered or not, producers often combine several
oils to form a blend—doing so achieves a balance of flavor and can
sometimes extend the oil's shelf life. If these products incorporate
oils from around the world, they're known as international blends.
On the other extreme, local farmers will sometimes pool their olives
or oil into one product, labeling it "cooperative."

In this globalized age, olives grown in one location (such as a
specific region in Spain) are often processed and bottled elsewhere.
In contrast, oils produced entirely on one estate (from olive to bottle)
are referred to as "estate-bottled."

# WHAT EXACTLY IS EXTRA VIRGIN OLIVE OIL?

Although olive oil comes in three main grades: "extra virgin," "virgin," and "pure" (or simply "olive oil"), we'll be focusing on extra virgin olive oil only—the most flavorful, healthful, and expensive olive oil.

Traditionally, both extra virgin and virgin olive oils have been produced without the use of chemicals or high heat (this makes them both "unrefined" and "cold-" or "expeller-pressed"). Since they're not treated or subjected to extreme temperatures, these oils retain more flavor, pigments, antioxidants, and vitamins.

Additionally, both extra virgin and virgin olive oils have historically been produced from the "first pressing" of the olives. After the first pressing, heat and sometimes chemicals are required to extract more oil from the olive paste. This reduces the quality of the oil, resulting in an inferior product.

So, how are extra virgin and virgin olive oils different? Extra virgin olive oil contains less free oleic acid (a monounsaturated fatty acid) than virgin or pure. While the International Olive Oil Council (IOOC) requires 0.8% or less, the California Olive Oil Council (COOC) stipulates 0.5% or less. Virgin olive oil, on the other hand, contains 1–3% acid. The term "acidity" is misleading, though, since these acids don't come across as astringency, but rather as greasiness and off flavors.

Along with having low acidity, extra virgin olive oil must taste fruity and flavorful (tasters look for a balance of bitterness, pungency, and fruitiness), with no defects in flavor or aroma, in tests conducted by organizations such as the IOOC.

Because pure olive oil contains both unrefined virgin olive oil and refined olive oil (oil that has been treated with chemicals and high heat to achieve clarity, a higher smoke point, and a longer shelf life), it has very little flavor. "Light" olive oil, a type of pure olive oil, has been refined to such a degree that it contains almost no flavor (incidentally, despite its moniker, it contains just as much fat as any other oil).

The end result? Virgin and pure olive oil have their uses—they're good for frying, baking, and sautéing. Yet, extra virgin olive oil is the only olive oil worth including in a tasting and drizzling on freshly toasted bread.

## Different Regions

As with wine, region means everything when it comes to olive oil—like grapes, olives are profoundly affected by climate. Different regions also grow different olives (each with a different flavor profile). For example, *kalamata* olives are popular in Greece, while *arbequina* olives are common in Spain. Different regions and countries also harvest their olives at different times. In Tuscany, the fruits are picked when they're under-ripe, resulting in deep green, peppery, and sometimes throat-catching oils, with green apple and artichoke flavors.

Acquiring knowledge of specific regions and olive varieties takes years. For now, just keep a few general rules in mind. Unlike Tuscan oils, oils from Liguria (the Italian Riviera) are delicate. Provençal oils are buttery, light, and floral; Spanish oils are golden, smooth, and fruity; and Greek oils are robust, green, and grassy, occasionally with a peppery aftertaste. Due to its many microclimates and olive varieties, Californian oils have an array of taste profiles.

Try to sample oil made with early-harvest olives. For these varieties, the olives are picked and pressed from September through November. Highly prized by experts, early-harvest oils taste pungent and grassy and contain much lower acidity levels than later presses.

## Deciphering the Label

As with all types of food and drink, the best way to pick the most delicious extra virgin olive oil is to taste. Many merchants allow you to sample their oils before buying. If you can't taste before you buy, at least make sure you purchase from a reputable merchant who is knowledgeable about olive oil, has high standards and turnover, and stores merchandise properly: out of direct light and in cool surroundings.

Producers who respect their oil will have bottled it in UV-protected packaging—dark or foil-wrapped glass containers or bottles. Avoid oils packaged in clear glass or plastic. The label should include information about the oil—the more details, the better. Most importantly, it should explicitly state "extra virgin olive oil."

Hunt for oils produced by famed olive oil regions or countries, such as Tuscany, Provence, California, and Greece. When looking at oils from a single country, try to find smaller brands that make regional, preferably estate-bottled oils, rather than generic "Italian" or "Greek" oils. Whereas "estate-bottled" tells you that the olives were grown and processed on one estate (with the resulting oil bottled there too), "product of Greece" is vague: the olives could have been grown and processed in Spain, and the resulting oil merely bottled in Greece. The labels "AOC" for France, "DOC" for Italy, and "DO" for Spain, are helpful, as they denote that the oils have been produced in a specific geographical area and feature regional characteristics.

Ideally, the label will also tell you which types of olives were used to produce the oil. If you see the words "hand-picked," that's definitely a good thing (hand-picking shows that the producer has taken a lot of care with the oil). "Stone-ground" means that the olives have been ground the old-fashioned way, with stones.

# STORING OLIVE OIL

Light and heat are the enemies of olive oil. Ideally, the substance should come in an airtight terra cotta, metal, or dark tinted glass container. If not, wrap the bottle in aluminum foil as soon as you can. Store your oil in a dark, cool place, not the sun-dappled countertop next to your hot stovetop.

Shelf-life is highly variable, depending on the type of olive, its ripeness when picked (early harvest oils last longer), whether it was filtered (filtered oils last longer— unfiltered should be used within one year of production), and how the olive oil was stored. New oils, since they decline over time, should be consumed quickly.

If stored properly, fresh extra virgin olive oil should last, on average, two years from the bottling date, or one year after opening. Refrigerating extra virgin olive oil is not necessary (doing so will cause it to congeal, although the fat will revert to a normal texture once it returns to room temperature). Finally, keep in mind that olive oil— even those that are initially very pungent and bitter—becomes milder with age.

# FIND YOUR
## EXTRA VIRGIN
# OLIVE OIL

To experience the full range of extra virgin olive oil color and flavor, start with a cross-tasting of products from Tuscany, Provence, Greece, California, Tunisia, Spain, or other famed olive oil areas. Later, to compare more similar samples, try oils from a single region, for example, Tuscany. In this type of tasting, you'll begin to note the nuances, such as grades of "peppery." You might also want to sample both late and early harvest oils, new oil, and filtered and unfiltered oils to understand the differences.

A couple of other interesting ideas: include one olive oil pressed with fruit, such as the blood orange extra virgin olive oil from the California company, O. Will you recognize the fruit flavor? You can even try comparing products made with a blend of olives to those produced with only one type of olive, such as the Greek *kalamata*—the latter are called "varietals."

### Shopping for Oil

One word of warning: be prepared to spend $100–$150 for six bottles of premium-quality extra virgin olive oil (each bottle can cost upwards of $15–$20). You can purchase high-quality oils at your nearest gourmet food shop, or from online merchants, such as www.chefshop.com, www.agferrari.com, www.eurogrocer.com, or www.oliviersandco.com. Other Web sources include www.zingermans.com, www.dibruno.com, www.levillage.com, www.formaggiokitchen.com, www.esperya.com, www.gustiamo.com, www.cybercucina.com, and www.deandeluca.com.

# CHOOSE YOUR
## ACCOMPANIMENTS

Before you begin tasting, set out an antipasto platter to enliven the palate—for example, with roasted red peppers, sun-dried tomatoes, olives, cheese, salami, and proscuitto. If you like, you can also prepare or purchase Mediterranean dips, such as hummus, baba ghanoush, and taramasalata. Have a nice bottle of Italian red wine open, such as a Sangiovese or, for a higher-end pick, a Brunello or a Super-Tuscan (a Cabernet-Sangiovese blend).

With the oils, serve small cubes of ciabatta (or slices of baguette) and *crudités* (raw vegetables) for dipping.

After the tasting, set out platters of biscotti and grapes, and pour some vin santo (Italian dessert wine) or brew some espresso. Alternatively, opt for fresh fruit and some dark chocolate.

### How to Assemble an Antipasto Platter

The antipasto platter is the ideal appetizer or snack: it's delicious and impressive-looking, yet requires almost no work to assemble and is most flavorful when served at room temperature. To create one yourself, select two or three types of prepared vegetable items, such as roasted red peppers; *pepperoncino*; sun-dried tomatoes; *cippolini agro dolce* (sweet and sour onions); marinated, cooked artichoke hearts; or mushrooms. Add to the shopping list two or three types of Italian (or even Spanish) cold meats, such as prosciutto, salami, soppressata, mortadella, and Serrano ham; olives; and cheeses, like Pecorino, ricotta salata, *bocconcini* (mini fresh mozzarella balls), and Parmigiano-Reggiano.

Whatever you choose, make sure to select high-quality products that encompass a range of colors and textures. With an eye for balance, arrange the items on a wide, preferably rustic platter. If you have a food-safe painted platter from Deruta, Italy, this is the perfect time to use it! Otherwise, consider a lazy susan (www.surlatable.com), divided platter, or the Fig Cena Fredda from Williams-Sonoma (www.williams-sonoma.com).

For additional color, garnish with sprigs of fresh herbs, such as thyme and rosemary. Place a serving fork or two alongside the platter for self-serving. Remember to also set out slices of ciabatta or another bread, and perhaps *grissini* (thin Italian breadsticks).

# COOKING: EXTRA VIRGIN OLIVE OIL

Generally, one shouldn't cook with premium-quality extra virgin olive oil—its taste and healthful properties diminish with heat. (Plus, extra virgin olive oil smokes at relatively low heat.) Instead, try pairing it with simple accompaniments, such as a fresh mozzarella, basil, and tomato salad; dips; cooked vegetables; or pasta. Alternatively, toast thin slices of a ciabatta or baguette in a 350°F oven until crispy and golden brown, about 15 minutes. Remove from the oven, drizzle generously with the oil, and sprinkle with sea salt. For another delicious snack, combine extra virgin olive oil, salt, and pomegranate molasses (available at Middle Eastern and Greek grocery stores) and serve with toasted pita bread.

To liven up mass-market extra virgin olive oil, try infusing it with a lemon flavor: just simmer the oil with some lemon peel (make sure to wash and dry the lemon and remove the white pith first) for about five minutes, then turn off the heat, and let sit, covered, for another ten minutes. Strain and pour into a bottle. Alternatively, prepare quick marinated olives: just drizzle some high-quality olives with your oil, add some fresh chopped herbs (such as thyme or oregano), minced garlic, red pepper flakes, and perhaps some freshly grated orange zest. Sprinkle with coarse salt and freshly ground black pepper, and let sit, covered, for two to three hours.

# MENU

AROUND-THE-WORLD EXTRA VIRGIN OLIVE OIL TASTING
(WEEKEND AFTERNOON)

## APPETIZER

SANGIOVESE

ANTIPASTO PLATTER *Roasted red peppers,* cippolini agro dolce *(sweet and sour onions), sun-dried tomatoes, olives, Pecorino Toscano, ricotta salata, proscuitto, salami*

## TASTING

SPANISH: AGUIBAL *Unfiltered oil made from arbequina olives, crushed within six hours of picking, maximum acidity 0.2%, harvest time and site of production on the label*

FRENCH (PROVENÇAL): A L'OLIVIER *Made by this producer since 1822*

PORTUGUESE: DOURO CARM "GRANDE ESCOLHA" *Unfiltered, organic, estate-grown and produced DOP oil, with barely 0.1% acidity, region and types of olives on the label*

CHILEAN: OLAVE *Organic, estate-produced and bottled oil with 0.15% acidity, types of olives on the label*

ITALIAN (TUSCAN): BADIA A COLTIBUONO *0.21% acidity, harvest and release times on the label*

CALIFORNIAN: MCEVOY RANCH *Organic, unfiltered, estate-grown, descriptions of orchard, olives, and methods of milling and extraction on the label*

## ACCOMPANIMENTS

*Vin santo (Italian dessert wine), seedess red grapes, and biscotti*

# ORGANIZE YOUR
# TASTING

Olive oil can be tasted in two ways: by itself, or with slices or cubes of unsalted white bread. Professionals sample extra virgin olive oil straight in small, lidded, dark glasses. The dark color ensures that testers won't be influenced by the oil's hue, and the lid holds in the volatile aromas. For at-home tasters, small plastic 1-ounce cups (available at party-supply stores) work best.

Although tasting the oil straight is the professional way, it's more palatable to sample it with bread and even *crudités* (raw vegetables). For the perfect compromise, try the product both by itself and as a condiment.

## What You'll Need

Before conducting the tasting, make sure to have on hand "The Basics" (see Chapter 1), as well as the materials below.

Note: Wine shouldn't be paired with olive oil, as its acidity interferes with the oil's taste and texture. If you serve wine with your pre-tasting accompaniments, switch to water for the tasting.

In front of each bottle of oil, stack enough small disposable plastic cups for each person tasting. You'll be pouring about a ½ tablespoon of each oil into each cup.

### MATERIALS

6 disposable 1-inch plastic cups per person

6 extra virgin olive oils, plus accompaniments, including ciabatta or other neutral-flavored white bread, the crusts removed and the bread cut into small cubes

Baby carrots and fennel slices

# LEARN YOUR
# PALATE

The color of olive oil does not reveal quality—many people are influenced by it and believe that darker means better, but that isn't necessarily the case. Rather, darker often means a stronger flavor, which may or may not suit you. In contrast, golden oils are usually more buttery, nutty, and mellow.

- •1• Place one of your hands over the cup and aerate the oil by swirling it around. Now, remove your hand, close your eyes, and bring the oil as close as possible to your nose, inhaling deeply a few times. What smells do you detect?

- •2• Sip about a quarter-teaspoon of the oil and slowly swirl it around from the front of your mouth and tongue along the sides, to the back, and to the palate and throat, without swallowing. Open your lips a bit and take short successive breaths, spreading the oil around your entire mouth. What flavors do you sense? Does the flavor change as the oil sits in your mouth?

- •3• Evaluate the oil's texture.

- •4• Either spit out or swallow the oil and consider its finish, or aftertaste. Is it long or short, meaning do the flavors dissipate quickly or last for a while in your mouth? What flavors remain?

- •5• Do you like this oil?

# TASTING GRID

As you taste each olive oil, write your answers to the questions on the previous page on a copy of this grid. Feel free to use the examples I provide below, and keep the grid as a record for future purchase.

| | ·1· | ·2· | ·3· | ·4· | ·5· | ·6· |
|---|---|---|---|---|---|---|
| **EXTRA VIRGIN OLIVE OIL NAME** | | | | | | |
| **AROMA** *Fruity, peppery, flowery, flat.* | | | | | | |
| **FLAVOR** *Opens with olive-fruity flavors, followed by pungent, bitter notes— with no "off" tastes. Negative: rancid, musty, winey, flat. Other terms: grassy, peppery, nutty, green, herbaceous, buttery, fragrant, mild, sweet, delicate, leafy.* | | | | | | |
| **TEXTURE** *Positive: Rich, heavy, thick, light, ethereal, smooth.* *Negative: greasy and astringent, leaving the mouth feeling puckery.* | | | | | | |
| **FINISH** *Mild, bitter, cough-in-ducing, peppery, sweet.* | | | | | | |
| **DO YOU LIKE IT?** | | | | | | |

# EXTRA VIRGIN OLIVE OIL
## *glossary*

**Artisan:** Made in small batches, usually with traditional methods.

**Blend:** Product comprising a blend of different oils.

**Cold- or Expeller-Pressed:** Oil pressed without high heat (room temperature warmth is now permitted by the IOOC)—a requirement for virgin and extra virgin oils.

**Cooperative:** Oil produced from a pool of local growers.

**Early Harvest:** Oil made from unripe olives; usually peppery, green, and pungent. (Later harvest oils are made from riper olives.)

**Estate-Bottled:** Entirely made on one estate, from picking to crushing to bottling.

**Extra Virgin Olive Oil:** Oil processed without chemicals or high heat. Traditionally made from the first pressing of the olives, these oils must undergo a chemical analysis and pass a sensory tasting by a panel of experts. Extra virgin olive oil must contain 0.8% or less free oleic acids (according to the IOOC, 0.5% or less according to the COOC), and should be fruity and flavorful, with no aroma or taste defects.

**Filtered:** Strained oil, meaning that all solids (fruit, leaves) have been removed, yielding a clearer product.

**First Press:** Traditionally, olive paste was pressed several times, with the first pressing yielding the highest quality oil. Today, the paste is most often pressed in a single centrifugal cycle, making the term virtually irrelevant.

**New Oil, *Aceite Nuevo*, or *Olio Nuevo*:** Young oil, which has not been set aside to settle; this difficult-to-find oil is often bitter and pungent (and delicious).

**Singe Varietal or Mono-Cultivar:** Oil made with just one type of olive, such as *kalamata*.

**Stone-Ground:** Oil for which olives were ground into a paste using 2-ton granite stones, a traditional method.

# CURED
# MEATS

*chapter eight*

Spicy, sweet, salty, fatty—what else could these words conjure up but salami, prosciutto, pepperoni, and other ready-to-eat cured meats? For hundreds of years, French charcuteries, Italian salumerias, German wurstmachers, and food artisans the world over have been transforming humble cuts of meat into preserved sausages and hams with just a bit of salt, spice, and know-how.

The best way to try meats you've never experienced before is through a tasting. Since cured meats are ready to serve, there's barely any work required on your part. Even better: cured meats are filling, meaning your tasting can take the place of a meal. Just begin with a salad or light hors d'oeuvres and appetizers; try the samples with some bread, cheese, and other accompaniments; and conclude with dessert. It couldn't be simpler, or more delicious!

# KNOW YOUR
# CURED MEATS

Cured meats have been called the oldest convenience food. Long before refrigeration—some say as far back as ancient Sumerian civilization, circa 3000 BC—our ancestors preserved meat to make it last, especially during long, hot summers. Today, the practice continues for a less practical reason: cured meats taste so good!

Curing techniques are virtually the same today as they were thousands of years ago, whether they're applied to a piece of meat (such as a ham, a pig's hind leg) or a mixture of ground meat, fat, and spices stuffed into casings (known as sausage).

In the first case, the meat is rubbed with salt or immersed in or injected with a salty solution called *brine*. Salting adds flavor, dries out the meat, and kills microbes. The flesh is further dehydrated through smoking, aging, or both. Since bacteria thrive in moist environments, drying the meat results in a longer shelf life.

For dry-cured sausages, the ground meat is mixed with fat, salt, sodium nitrate, a live culture, sugar, and spices, such as paprika. Sodium nitrate lends flavor, preserves fresh meat's reddish color, and helps to combat botulism, a severe, sometimes fatal food poisoning. Meanwhile, the live culture encourages fermentation; in this process, chemical changes brought about by enzymes help add flavor to the meat.

After combining, this mixture is stuffed into casings. Traditionally, these are the large intestines of pigs or sheep, but now they often take the form of collagen or cellulose. Finally, the sausages are salted, fermented, sometimes smoked, and hung to dry in a roughly 55–60° F environment with 60–70% humidity.

## Classifying Cured Meats

There are hundreds, if not thousands, of varieties of cured meat. This bounty is not surprising given how many variables come into play. To get a sense of the differentiating factors, consider the following questions: First, what types and breeds of animals were used? Where were the animals raised, what did they eat, and how were they slaughtered? Which cuts of meat were included in the finished product? For sausages, were the meat and fat coarsely or finely chopped? Were all the tough sinews and tendons removed? What spices were added, and in what quantities? What was the proportion of lean meat to fat? What type of casing was used? For cured cuts of meat, was the meat rubbed with fat, oil, or spices? Was it smoked or air-dried? For how long? What was the overall aging time?

## Sausage Terminology

Of course, many other types of sausages—beyond dry or cured—exist. Here's the low-down: Cooked sausages have been fully cooked and must be eaten immediately or refrigerated. Cooked smoked sausages, which have also been cooked—partially by smoking—may be eaten hot or cold and should be refrigerated. Fresh sausages are completely raw and must be cooked and refrigerated. In Germany, sausages are classified as raw (which sometimes means cured), cooked, or pre-cooked.

### *Classified* CURED MEATS KEY

✳ **CURED HAM**
The pig's hind leg (called a ham) has been cured.

⊞ **OTHER CURED CUTS OF MEAT**
Other parts of the animal (such as its fat or loin) have been cured.

⊞ **DRY OR CURED SAUSAGE**
Ground meat is mixed with fat, spices, a live culture, and other ingredients, then stuffed into casings. The raw sausages are then cured.

| · NAME · | · TYPE · | · COUNTRY · | · CHARACTERISTICS · |
|---|---|---|---|
| ❋ Prosciutto di Parma | Pork | Italy | Salted, stored in cold rooms, brushed, resalted, aged, rinsed, beaten with mallets, hung in warmer rooms, rubbed with pork fat, salt, and pepper, aged again; matured a total of 10 months–2 years |
| ❋ Culatello | Pork | Italy | Air-dried for at least 9 months |
| ❋ Serrano | Pork | Spain | Salt-cured, stored in cold rooms, hung in cold rooms, then warmer rooms, where they're matured for at least 1 year |
| ❋ Speck Trentino-Alto Aldige | Pork | Italy | Dry-salted, smoked, and aged for 5–6 months |
| ❋ Yorkshire (York) | Pork | United Kingdom | Dry-salted and sometimes smoked |
| ❋ Westphalian | Pork | Germany | Rubbed with salt, brined, desalted, cold-smoked, then dried |
| ❋ Bayonne | Pork | France | Rubbed with salt, saltpeter, sugar, pepper, and herbs and dried for 4–6 months |
| ❋ Smithfield or Country | Pork | United States | Salt-cured and smoked |
| ⊞ Lomo | Pork | Italy and Spain | Boneless pork loin, salted, spiced, and air-dried |
| ⊞ Bresaola | Beef, horse, veal, or venison | Italy | Salted, spiced, and air-dried or smoked |
| ⊞ Sopressata | Pork | Italy | Pork cuttings flavored with red wine, pepper, and garlic, then stuffed and pressed |
| ⊞ Finocchiona | Pork | Italy | Coarse-ground pork and fat, flavored with fennel seeds |
| ⊞ Salamino Piccante (called pepperoni in the USA) | Pork (and sometimes beef) | Italy | Flavored with red pepper |
| ⊞ Salame Toscano | Pork and beef | Italy | Coarse-ground, flavored with peppercorns |
| ⊞ Cacciatore ("hunter's" sausage) | Pork, sometimes wild boar | Italy | Flavored with garlic, black pepper, and sometimes red wine, then dry-cured |
| ⊞ Zungenwurst | Pork | Germany | Consists of diced lean pork, blood, and tongue |
| ⊞ Salami de Strasbourg | Beef (meat) and pork (fat) | France | Thin, smoked |
| ⊞ Rosette de Lyon | Pork | France | Made with pork leg meat |
| ⊞ Chorizo (Note: Many types exist. Keep in mind that Mexican chorizo—which is fresh—is entirely different.) | Pork | Spain | Coarsely cut pork and pork fat flavored with garlic and smoked paprika |

# FIND YOUR
## CURED MEATS

For your tasting, serve products from all over the world or stick with one country or region, such as Italy or the Mediterranean. Either way, aim for variety: include sliced cured ham and dried sausages, mild as well as spicy products.

All that being said, try not to fixate on finding specific varieties of meat. For one thing, you might get confused, as the same names are often used to describe very different products. Case in point: the Italian term "bresaola" can be applied to air-dried beef, horse, veal, or venison!

Making things even more complicated, many meats can only be found in specific countries, regions, or even towns. A primary reason for this limitation is the law: some countries prohibit the importation of cured meat items that have not been, among other factors, aged in high-tech temperature- and humidity-controlled environments. In response, several producers, especially in Italy, are installing new curing rooms, so that their products will meet these standards. In the meantime, domestic producers have been turning out approximations of the "real thing."

Finally, if your local gourmet shop or ethnic market doesn't offer cured hams by the slice, you'll probably need to bypass ham altogether—you definitely won't want to spend $70–$300 on a whole ham when you only need a few pieces! For the same reason, try sticking with cured sausages that you can find in smaller sizes or quantities.

## Shopping for Cured Meats

You can find cured meat products at gourmet chains; grocers with Internet sites, such as www.dartagnan.com and www.igourmet.com; and specialty stores, including Salumi Artisan Meats in Washington State, which offers innovative products, such as sausages flavored with fennel, pepper, and curry or chocolate, cinnamon, and ancho and chipotle peppers. Seek out ethnic markets; if they don't carry cured meat products, ask them who does—you never know what you might discover!

According to some estimates, Germany produces over 1,200 types of sausage, with Britain coming in at over 470!

Wherever you shop, look for the terms "smoked and cured meats," "charcuterie," and "salumi." Ask for help, and make sure that the products you purchase are cured. Dried sausages are firmer and often darker in color than their fresh counterparts. If you see sausages that are *not* refrigerated, they're probably dried. Finally, read the wrapper, which might tell you how to prepare, serve, and store the product.

To find high-quality dried sausages, look for aromatic products prepared with natural casings. If you see a bit of dry white-gray mold on the exterior, don't turn away—many experts consider this to be a must for superior dried sausages. In the event that you're able to sample products, make sure that the meat, rather than the spices, is the primary flavor.

On the other hand, avoid products with fuzzy or green mold, tough white sinew and tendons, or a greasy feeling. By the same token, an excess of fillers, such as flour, soy protein, dry milk, and cereals, can mean that the producer wasn't generous with meat. Likewise, an extensive ingredient list, with artificial colors, MSG, preservatives, and water, reveals that the product is not "the real thing."

Since sausages should be sliced very thinly, preferably with an electric meat slicer, you might want to ask the store to do the cutting for you. If so, have them leave a small piece of each sausage unpeeled and unsliced, so your guests can see its exterior.

To find the most flavorful ham, look for larger, older cured legs and meat still on the bone. Have it hand-sliced thinly and make sure that your portion includes plenty of fat, which is considered the best part by many.

Overall, plan on serving ½-ounce of each meat per taster (double that amount for meal-time tastings).

## OTHER WEB SOURCES

Other places to shop for cured meats online are:

- www.agferrari.com
- www.deanandeluca.com
- www.dibruno.com
- www.esperya.com
- www.eurogrocer.com
- www.formaggiokitchen.com
- www.laespanolameats.com
- www.salumicuredmeats.com
- www.spanishtable.com
- www.tienda.com
- www.zingermans.com

# STORING CURED MEATS

Since cured meats are so delicious, it's easy to forget that they were invented for a utilitarian reason: long-term storage. Thus, keeping them in good condition is a cinch. Wrapped unsliced dry sausages can last for up to one year in the refrigerator; unrefrigerated, they can keep for up to 3 months. To maintain their moisture in your refrigerator's dry environment, try wrapping them in a damp cloth and placing them in the vegetable bin. Sliced dry sausage or cured ham should be tightly wrapped and placed in the refrigerator for up to 2 weeks, or sometimes even longer. While these general guidelines cover most meats, always check the wrapper for additional information, as it can vary from product to product.

# CHOOSE YOUR
## ACCOMPANIMENTS

The food and drinks you enjoy during your tasting should match the meats you're trying. The easiest way to ensure this is to stay within a country. For instance, for an Italian-themed evening, begin with a glass of Chianti. Go with beer if you're focusing on German meats, Rioja or dry sherry if your theme is Spain, and Côtes-du-Rhône if you're focusing on France.

Since the meats are heavy, have a light Greek salad or *crudités* before the tasting. You could also start with warm and crispy Robbiola Toasts with Fresh Oregano (see page 173).

During the tasting, serve bread, cheese, vegetables, condiments, and fruit—ideally, the appropriate accompaniments for each country. For example, with French samples, try cornichons, mustard, and a Beaujolais; with Italian meats, set out Pecorino cheese, fennel, fresh figs, and a Barbera. (In particular, Italian hams are delicious with *mostarda*, whole fruits in a mustard-laced syrup.) For Spanish samples, opt for Spanish cheeses, such as Manchego or Zamorano, along with quince paste, Marcona almonds, and arbequina olives. Serve a Ribera del Duero wine alongside it.

Keep within your theme for dessert as well. For a Spanish tasting, try Spanish Chocolate Toasts (see page 173). If your theme is Italy, consider making my twist on one of the country's most popular treats: Hazelnut Tiramisu (see page 174).

On the other hand, if you decide to throw an "Around the World" cured meat tasting, choose appropriate accompaniments for each sample, like Spanish cheeses and olives with the Spanish meats, and Italian cheeses and olives with the Italian meats.

# MENU

### Italian Cured Meat Tasting
### (Weekend lunch-time)

## APPETIZER

CHIANTI

ORANGE AND RADICCHIO SALAD WITH LEMON PARSLEY VINAIGRETTE

ROBBIOLA TOASTS WITH FRESH OREGANO

## TASTING

CHIANTI

BRESAOLA

PROSCIUTTO DI PARMA

CACCIATORE

FINOCCHIONA

SALAME TOSCANO

SOPPRESSATA

## ACCOMPANIMENTS

*Ciabatta slices, Pecorino and Parmigiano-Reggiano cheeses, extra virgin olive oil, salt, pepper, radishes, sliced fennel, and green olives*

## DESSERT

*Hazelnut Tiramisu*

# RECIPES FOR ACCOMPANIMENTS

These simple, rustic toasts—the first inspired by Italy and the second a popular snack in Spain—couldn't be more delicious. And who can resist tiramisu for dessert?

## ROBBIOLA TOASTS WITH FRESH OREGANO

### MAKES 16

*If you can't find Robbiola, use Taleggio, Fontina, or even Brie. Baguette slices can be substituted for the ciabatta, and thyme or marjoram for the oregano. I love to use a Tuscan extra virgin olive oil and gray sea salt for these toasts.*

- **1.** Preheat the oven to 300°F. Place the bread slices on two foil-lined baking sheets, and transfer to the middle rack of the oven. Bake until crisp and a bit golden, about 10 minutes. Remove from the oven.

- **2.** Using a butter knife, spread each piece of cheese over each piece of bread, and sprinkle with the oregano. Return to the oven until the cheese melts, about 7 minutes.

- **3.** Take out of the oven. Drizzle each toast with ½ teaspoon of olive oil, and then sprinkle with a pinch of sea salt. Serve immediately.

16 ½-inch-thick slices ciabatta

8 ounces Robbiola cheese, cut into 16 slices

2 tablespoons finely chopped fresh oregano leaves

2 tablespoons plus 2 teaspoons high-quality, peppery extra virgin olive oil

Sea salt to taste

## SPANISH CHOCOLATE TOASTS

### MAKES 16

*I love to use a Spanish extra virgin olive oil and gray sea salt here. There's no need to go for a very expensive chocolate—any dark chocolate will do.*

- **1.** Preheat the oven to 300°F. Place the bread slices on two foil-lined baking sheets, and drizzle each with 1 teaspoon of the oil. Transfer to the middle rack of the oven and bake until crisp and a bit golden, about 10 minutes. Remove from the oven.

- **2.** Divide the chocolate among the toasts. Then, return to the oven until the chocolate melts, about 7 minutes.

- **3.** Take out of the oven and, with a butter knife, spread the melted chocolate all over each toast. Sprinkle with a pinch of sea salt and serve immediately.

16 ½-inch-thick slices ciabatta or baguette

5 tablespoons plus 1 teaspoon high-quality extra virgin olive oil

1 pound dark chocolate, coarsely chopped

Sea salt to taste

## HAZELNUT TIRAMISU

SERVES 8-10

*If, like me, you don't own an espresso machine, just visit your nearest coffee shop for some shots (or use strong coffee). Feel free to substitute another liqueur (such as Amaretto or Kahlua) for the Frangelico. Note: since this recipe contains raw eggs, do not offer it to anyone with a compromised immune system.*

*Serving dish: 3-quart, 13x9x2-inch rectangle. (If you use a dish with another volume, you'll need different quantities of ingredients, especially cookies.)*

1 cup hazelnuts*, skinned

¾ cup plus 1 tablespoon white or granulated sugar, divided

2½ ounces bittersweet chocolate in bar form (since the espresso is bitter, go with a high-sugar bar)

¾ cup plus 6 tablespoons Frangelico (hazelnut liqueur), divided

2½ cups plus 2 tablespoons (unsweetened) espresso, or strong coffee, (about 27 shots), cooled

6 large eggs

3 cups mascarpone cheese (from 3 8-oz packages)

32 savoiardi ladyfinger cookies, about 9 ounces

1 teaspoon unsweetened cocoa powder, divided

* Make sure not to purchase giant hazelnuts.

•1• Note: Only follow this step if your hazelnuts have not already been skinned: Preheat the oven to 400°F. Place the nuts on a baking sheet and, once the oven is preheated, toast for 8–10 minutes. Remove, let cool for 15 minutes, and—using a cloth towel—rub the nuts, removing their skins. (Some skins may remain.)

•2• With a food processor (a small version is best), grind the nuts with 1 tablespoon of the sugar until a fine powder forms, about 10 seconds.

•3• With a vegetable peeler, shave the chocolate (as you would peel a carrot) to form curls (it helps if the chocolate is room temperature or warmer).

•4• In a bowl, combine ¾ cup of the Frangelico with all of the cooled espresso.

•5• Separate the eggs, discarding two of the whites. Using a standing mixer (with the whisk attachment) or a hand-mixer, at medium-high speed, beat the four remaining egg whites with 2 tablespoons of the sugar, until soft peaks form, about 2–3 minutes.

•6• Also with a standing or hand mixer (in another bowl) and at medium-high speed, beat the six egg yolks with the remaining 10 tablespoons sugar until the mixture becomes thick and pale cream in color, about 2 minutes.

•**7**• Add the mascarpone, ground nuts, and remaining 6 tablespoons of Frangelico to the egg-yolk mixture, stirring until fully incorporated. Then, with a rubber spatula, gently fold in the egg whites, mixing until thoroughly blended (but do not over-mix, as you want to retain the aeration of the egg whites).

•**8**• One at a time, dip each cookie in the Frangelico-espresso mixture, about 2 seconds per side (you don't want them to absorb too much liquid and lose their structure) then lay them in the bottom of the serving dish. Continue doing this, creating a bottom layer in your serving dish (you should use about 20 of the cookies). Once you've covered the bottom, spoon one half of the mascarpone mixture on top. With a tea ball or small sifter, sift over ½ teaspoon of the cocoa powder. Sprinkle with one half of the chocolate shavings. Repeat once more, this time using fewer cookies (about 12), then the mascarpone mixture, and finally the cocoa and chocolate. Note: You might have some leftover Frangelico-espresso mixture.

•**9**• Refrigerate for at least 30 minutes and serve. (This dessert is delicious up to 3 days after preparation.)

# ORGANIZE YOUR
# TASTING

To match the ambiance to the food, you might want to decorate the table in a rustic or "farmhouse" fashion, with wooden boards and homemade pottery. Most importantly, though, don't forget the red wine, crusty bread, and other accompaniments. You're going for a bounty of flavors, textures, and colors.

Place six plates in the middle of your table, one plate for each type of meat sample. Take the meat out of the refrigerator 30 minutes to 1 hour before the tasting, giving it a chance to rise to room temperature (at which it should be tasted).

If your sausages haven't yet been peeled and sliced, use a thin-bladed knife to peel them and a sharp chef's knife or an electric meat slicer to slice them—the latter you can find for about $100 and experts swear by it. Regardless of your method, remove the exterior mold and cut the slices thinly, leaving a bit of the sausage intact, so your guests can observe the exterior.

## WHAT YOU'LL NEED

Before conducting the tasting, make sure to have on hand "The Basics" (see Chapter 1), along with the materials listed at right.

Place each type of cured meat on a plate, identifying it with a label or a folded index card.

MATERIALS

Knives

Six plates

Appropriate cured meats and accompaniments

# LEARN YOUR
# PALATE

First, sample each meat by itself. Then, try it with the appropriate accompaniments—you might want to offer your guests recommendations, based on traditional pairings. For example, bresaola is served with extra virgin olive oil, Alto Adige speck with pickled gherkins and unsalted butter, and (in Italy's Liguria region), *coppa* (cured pork shoulder) with fava beans and Pecorino cheese. Meanwhile, in Italy's Veneto region, a large salame, called *soppressata*, is often paired with freshly ground horseradish pickled in white wine vinegar.

- •**1**• Observe the meat and describe its diameter (if it's a sausage) and color. (If it's a sausage, make sure also to examine the unpeeled, unsliced piece.) While natural casing and some exterior mold are positive sightings, you don't want to see any interior mold or bloody spots.

- •**2**• Hold up the meat in front of your nose and inhale. How would you describe its aroma?

- •**3**• Bite down and chew on a piece of the meat. What flavors are you experiencing? Are they mild or strong, spicy or sweet? Ideally, the flavor should be balanced, and not bland or overly salty.

- •**4**• What is the texture of the meat? Is it soft or firm? (Excessive hardness or toughness can mean that meat is over the hill or was over-aged.) If the sample is a dry sausage, is the meat finely or coarsely ground?

- •**5**• Do you like the product? Would you purchase it?

# TASTING GRID

As you taste each sample, ask yourself the questions on the previous page and write your answers on a copy of this grid. Feel free to use the tasting terms provided below, and keep this grid as a record for future purchases.

| | ·1· | ·2· | ·3· | ·4· | ·5· | ·6· |
|---|---|---|---|---|---|---|
| **CURED MEAT NAME** | | | | | | |
| **APPEARANCE** *Diameter, if relevant. Color. Mold.* | | | | | | |
| **AROMA** *Mild, strong, peppery, spicy, herbal, salty, nutty, fruity, earthy.* | | | | | | |
| **FLAVOR** *Mild or strong. Black pepper, cayenne, paprika, cinnamon, nutty, salty, herbal. Sweet or balanced.* | | | | | | |
| **TEXTURE** *Soft, firm, hard, tough, fine- or coarse-ground, fatty, smooth, lean, gritty, wet, dry, greasy, chewy.* | | | | | | |
| **DO YOU LIKE IT?** | | | | | | |

# CURED MEATS
## *glossary*

**Brine:** A salty solution used for preserving and pickling various foods.

**Casings:** Tubular membranes into which meat is stuffed for sausages; traditionally made from pig or sheep intestine, but now more commonly collagen or cellulose.

**Cellulose:** A complex carbohydrate made up of glucose; a main component of plant cell walls and used in the manufacture of some sausages, pharmaceuticals, and other products.

**Charcuterie:** Cooked or processed meats, such as pâté or sausages; a shop specializing in such foods.

**Collagen:** A fibrous protein present in bone, cartilage, and tendons.

**Cure:** To preserve food, through salting, smoking, aging, and pickling or corning (soaking in brine).

**Fermentation:** Chemical changes brought about by enzymes.

**Ham:** The hind leg of a pig, usually from the middle of the shank to the hip; available fresh, cooked, or cured.

**Nitrates and Nitrites:** Types of salt that preserve meat; considered by many to be unhealthy if consumed in large quantities.

# BALSAMIC VINEGAR

---

*chapter nine*

Vinegar might seem an odd choice for a tasting, given the pucker-inducing acidity of most varieties. Yet, authentic balsamic vinegar is quite unlike its brethren: while most vinegar is made from wine, balsamic vinegar is produced exclusively from *grape must* (unfermented grape juice).

The end result is thick and syrupy, simultaneously sweet and slightly acidic, and highly complex, evoking fruit, wood, and spices. It's not surprising, then, that true balsamic vinegar is extremely expensive, a veritable luxury item. Fortunately, versions exist at many price ranges, allowing us all to experience a substance so good that it was limited to Italian nobility until very recently. Why not open up your own *palazzo* and invite some friends and family over for a truly decadent balsamic vinegar tasting?

# KNOW YOUR
# BALSAMIC
# VINEGAR

According to Italian law, true balsamic vinegar, or *Aceto Balsamico Tradizionale*, can only be produced in two provinces (Modena and Reggio Emilia, both in the Northern Italian region of Emilia-Romagna) using specific local varieties of grapes. After harvesting, the grapes are pressed, and the resulting must is filtered. The must is cooked over an open flame for 12 to 40 hours until it's reduced to 70–30% of its original volume. It is then set aside to ferment and *acetify* (become vinegar) in a wooden or metal container, for anywhere from two months to four years.

At this point, the cooked must enters the *batteria* (battery), a series of barrels in various sizes and of different woods, among them oak, ash, mulberry, cherry, and chestnut. The liquid first enters the largest barrel. Next, it is transferred to at least two other barrels, in descending size order. The total aging period is at least 12 years, and sometimes as long as 100 years! During this time, the balsamic reduces in volume, which concentrates its flavor and results in a thick, sweet, multidimensional product.

As simple as it sounds, there's more to making Tradizionale than just aging juice. At no point is any barrel more than 75% full, since the vinegar requires air to properly age. In addition, no more than about 10–20% of the total vinegar in the battery is released each year. As a result, vinegars of different ages mix together in the barrels, meaning that a bottle of Tradizionale purchased today might include some vinegar that is several decades old.

Even if a product has been prepared according to the above process, it still may not earn the assignment *Tradizionale*. It must first pass a taste test by one of two Tradizionale consortia for Modena or Reggio Emilia. If the substance doesn't meet specific scoring minimums, it's designated *Condimento* or *Aceto Balsamico in Corso di Invecchiomento* (meaning "in the process of aging") and sold at a lower price, aged longer and then retested, or heavily diluted and mixed with other ingredients to become commerical grade (see below). Only after passing this taste test can Tradizionale be packaged—either as Aceto Balsamico Tradizionale di Modena or Aceto Balsamico Tradizionale di Reggio Emilia— usually in a 100-milliliter bottle.

## The World Outside of Tradizionale

All balsamics not deemed Tradizionale are considered *Aceto Balsamico di Modena* or *Industriale*. Since no overall standards for this category are in place, these products are of extremely variable quality. Generally, the choicest bottles among them are made exclusively with cooked must. If not, they at least include cooked must, with the addition of wine vinegar (try to avoid products with caramel coloring or flavoring or caramelized sugar).

The longer the aging process and the more time the balsamic spends in wooden barrels, the better. Yet, many bottles aren't aged at all. Even if they are, their exposure to wood might come merely from mixing with wood chips or steeping in giant wooden barrels. In the latter case, much of the liquid might not even come in contact with the wood.

At least you'll know that vinegars labeled "CABM" (which stands for *Consorzio Aceto Balsamico di Modena*) include must only from grapes from the Emilia-Romagna region, and have been produced and bottled in Modena. Nevertheless, CABM, founded in 1993, is made up mostly of large producers, which generally do not follow the traditional method; the result, in my opinion, is that their balsamics are not always high quality.

The cheapest balsamic vinegar is thin and acidic—the substance you find in many salad dressings. These products can be bottled anywhere, even in the United States. In 2002, a private association, the *Assaggiatori Italiani Balsamico* (Association of Italian Balsamic Tasters, or AIB) instituted a four-leaf quality designation system to help consumers differentiate among the products. Unfortunately, it is neither an official nor recommended method for evaluating balsamics.

It is helpful in suggesting applications for the different grades of balsamic vinegar. Less expensive products should be used for salad dressings, marinades, and sauces, while more expensive balsamics are "condiments," meant to be drizzled over fresh vegetables, cheeses, meats, and fish. The most premium products are true "finishers," intended for drizzling over strawberries or gelato or even drinking straight.

It takes at least nine years to complete the requisite certification courses to become a master taster of Tradizionale.

# STORING BALSAMIC VINEGAR

Balsamic vinegar couldn't be easier to store: ideally, keep the bottle tightly closed and in a cool, dark place. It lasts forever, gradually evaporating and concentrating in flavor. So, if you invest in several expensive bottles, you'll be able to enjoy them for years to come.

## IT'S ALL ABOUT GRADES

Few subjects seem as impenetrable as balsamic vinegar. To remedy this situation, the chart on the next page is a veritable balsamic vinegar cheat-sheet, generally classifying the different grades from highest to lowest (though Tradizionale from Modena and Reggio Emilia are equally regarded). Keep in mind that the colors in parentheses are found on the labels.

## ... AND PRICE

Before you have a heart attack from balsamic prices, I highly recommend splitting the cost of this tasting with others. Consider this event a true splurge and, afterwards, just divide the bottles amongst the group. To keep the costs down, you can also just limit your tasting to four to five, rather than six, samples.

The good news is that although Tradizionale bottles cost around $140–$180 for 25-year and $75–$90 for 12-year, high quality non-Tradizionale vinegars are much more reasonably priced, averaging around $20–$30.

## Classified
### BALSAMIC VINEGAR KEY

**⊞✻ ACETO BALSAMICO TRADIZIONALE**

This vinegar has only one ingredient, grape must, and is labeled with the words *Aceto Balsamico Tradizionale*. It's made exclusively in the districts of Modena and Reggio-Emilia. Generally, the longer the aging time, the better and more expensive the product.

**⊞ REGGIO-EMILIA**

Look for tall, thin 100- and 250-ml glass bottles with corks sealed in red wax. The labels should contain the words "Reggio-Emilia" and "Consorzio Produttori."

**✻ MODENA**

Look for 100-ml bottles in the shape of a globe mounted on a stand. Each bottle has a gold- or ivory-colored capsule over the cork, a picture of an antique jug, and a serial number. Look for the words "Modena," "Sigillo di Garanzia Consorzio Produttori," and "antico condimento."

**⊞ ACETO BALSAMICO DI MODENA (OR INDUSTRIALE)**

This category extends to all bottles not considered Tradizionale—quality differs markedly. Products labeled "CABM" include must only from grapes in the Emilia-Romagna region, and have been produced and bottled in Modena. If you come across bottles labeled with the (rarely used) 4-leaf designation system, a 4-leaf means higher quality, while a 1-leaf means the lower quality.

| · TYPE · | · CHARACTERISTICS · |
|---|---|
| ⊞ Bollino Oro or Extravecchio (gold) | Aged at least 25 years |
| ⊞ Bollino Argento (silver) | Aged up to 25 years (minimum 17–20 years) |
| ⊞ Bollino Aragosta (lobster-red) | Aged at least 12 years |
| ✳ Extravecchio (gold) | Aged at least 25 years |
| ✳ Vecchio (ivory) | Aged at least 12 years |
| ⊞ CABM Invecchiato (aged) (white) | Aged at least 3 years in wooden casks or barrels |
| ⊞ CABM Affinato (matured) (red) | Matured up to 3 years in wooden containers |
| ⊞ Four leaves | Used for drizzling and drinking straight, as a digestif |
| ⊞ Three leaves | Used for drizzling over fish and meat, ice cream, cheese, and strawberries |
| ⊞ Two leaves | Used for salad dressings, marinades, and sauces |
| ⊞ One leaf | Used for salad dressings |

# FIND YOUR
# BALSAMIC
# VINEGAR

To get to know the various grades of balsamic, I recommend opting for bottles in a few categories. For example, include a 12-year, 20-year, and 30-year Tradizionale, as well as two to three of the highest-quality non-Tradizionale balsamics you can find. If you come across them, try purchasing lower-grade or younger balsamics made by Tradizionale producers, such as the Aceto Balsamico di Modena "Vecchio" from Acetaia Pedroni, available from www.agferrari.com; as of 2005, the 250-milliliter bottle retails for $49.99. Usually high-quality, these cost much less than Tradizionale vinegars.

At the other extreme, if you're a true balsamic vinegar connoisseur (with extremely deep pockets), try featuring only Tradizionale products, comparing the two levels from Modena to the three from Reggio Emilia. Unfortunately, it generally isn't worth venturing into the under $15-per-bottle zone for tastings—such vinegars are perfect for cooking, but are too acidic to be palatable on their own.

## Shop for Balsamic Vinegars

When shopping, read the labels carefully. For example, if you'd like to purchase Tradizionale, make sure that the label states "Aceto Balsamico Tradizionale."

Try to order from reputable online merchants, including www.agferrari.com (which offers an incredible selection), www.zingermans.com, and www.eurogrocer.com. Other Web sources are www.chefshop.com, www.cybercucina.com, www.dibruno.com, www.formaggiokitchen.com, and www.igourmet.com.

# CHOOSE YOUR
## ACCOMPANIMENTS

Start your tasting with a glass of light Italian white wine, such as Pinot Grigio, and a slice of Frittata with Peas, Pancetta, Fresh Mint, and Pecorino (a frittata is an open-face baked omelet—see page 195 for the recipe), some salad, and perhaps some Salami Chips (see technique below). Serve the first few vinegars with slices of neutral-flavored bread (such as baguette or ciabatta) and Parmigiano-Reggiano cheese. Drizzle the next-to-last sample over strawberries and perhaps some vanilla ice cream, and drink the last sample straight—it's frequently taken as a digestif in Italy.

## SALAMI CHIPS

The idea for this delicious, easy appetizer comes from the September 2004 issue of *Gourmet* Magazine. It's best to prepare these chips right before you begin your tasting.

Have the salami (I prefer Genoa) cut into 32 paper-thin slices (about five ounces total) for you at the store. If that's not possible, make sure to slice the meat as thinly as you can. Then preheat the oven to 375°F. Arrange the salami slices in a single layer on two foil-lined baking sheets and place on the middle rack of the preheated oven. Bake until the side facing up is a bit crispy, about five minutes. Then, using tongs, turn the slices over. Continue baking until that side is also slightly crispy, about another five minutes. With your tongs, transfer the salami chips to paper towel-lined baking sheets or plates, and serve warm or at room temperature.

# MENU

VARIED BALSAMIC TASTING

(WEEKEND AFTERNOON)

## APPETIZER

PINOT GRIGIO

FRITTATA WITH PEAS, PANCETTA, FRESH MINT, AND PECORINO

SALAMI CHIPS

## TASTING

THREE OF THE HIGHEST-QUALITY (PREFERABLY AGED)
NON-TRADIZIONALE BALSAMIC VINEGARS YOU CAN FIND

TRADIZIONALE VECCHIO

TRADIZIONALE BOLLINO ARGENTO

TRADIZIONALE EXTRAVECCHIO

## ACCOMPANIMENTS

*Ciabatta slices, Parmigiano-Reggiano, fresh strawberries, vanilla gelato*

## FRITTATA WITH PEAS, PANCETTA, FRESH MINT, AND PECORINO

### SERVES 6

*This versatile dish is delicious as an hors d'oeuvre (when sliced into small wedges), as well as for brunch, lunch, or a light dinner. Feel free to vary the fillings to create your own variation. If you can't find pancetta (rolled Italian cured bacon), just use bacon. Parmigiano-Reggiano is an excellent substitution for Pecorino (a firm Italian sheep's milk cheese). Use an inexpensive extra virgin olive oil for this recipe.*

•**1**• Preheat the oven to 375°F. Whisk the eggs with ¼ teaspoon of salt and about 4 turns of black pepper until well-blended.

•**2**• Heat 1 tablespoon of oil in a 10-inch oven-safe nonstick skillet over medium heat. Once hot, add the pancetta cubes and cook, stirring occasionally, until a bit crisp and slightly darker, about 3 to 4 minutes. Spoon the pancetta from the pan and set aside. Pour out the fat and, off the heat, carefully wipe out the pan.

•**3**• Add the remaining 1 tablespoon of oil to the pan, then the shallots and garlic, and sauté over medium heat until the shallots are slightly softened and translucent, about 2 minutes.

•**4**• Add the peas, the other ¼ teaspoon of salt, and lemon zest, and sauté for 1 minute, stirring. Return the pancetta cubes to the pan and stir, spreading out the mixture with the back of your spoon.

•**5**• Pour in the eggs and shake the pan to level the ingredients. Sprinkle the top with the grated Pecorino, and grind with about 4 turns of pepper. Continue cooking on the stovetop until the eggs begin to set, about 2 minutes. Then transfer to the upper rack of the oven until the eggs are puffed and dry, about 20 minutes.

•**6**• With a spatula, loosen the edges of the frittata, and slide it onto a plate. Sprinkle the fresh mint leaves on top. Serve hot, cold, or at room temperature.

6 large eggs

½ teaspoon coarse salt, divided

Freshly ground black pepper to taste

2 tablespoons extra virgin olive oil, divided

2½ ounces pancetta, cut into ¼-inch dice (½ cup)

3–4 large shallots, thinly sliced (1 cup)

1 teaspoon pressed or minced garlic (about 1 large clove)

About 9¼ ounces frozen green peas (2 cups), slightly defrosted

1 teaspoon freshly grated lemon zest (from 1 lemon)

¼ cup plus 2 tablespoons coarsely grated Pecorino cheese (about 1½ ounces)

2 tablespoons chopped fresh mint leaves

# ORGANIZE YOUR
# TASTING

You'll be tasting these samples in order from the lowest-grade to the highest-grade—the first few with cheese and bread, the next-to-last over strawberries and ice cream, and the final one alone. In between, you'll want to cleanse your palate with bread and water. While professionals observe vinegars against a flashlight or the flame of a candle to gauge specific coloring, density, and clarity, you're going to be a bit more low-key!

## WHAT YOU'LL NEED

Before conducting the tasting, make sure to have on hand "The Basics" (see Chapter 1), as well as the materials listed below. Don't forget the bread, Parmigiano-Reggiano or Pecorino cheese, strawberries, and vanilla gelato or ice cream.

In front of each bottle of vinegar, stack enough small cups (disposable, plastic ones are easy for cleanup) for each taster (for example, for an 8-person tasting of 6 vinegars, you'll need a total of 48 cups—6 stacks of 8). You'll be pouring about ½–1 teaspoon of each sample into each cup.

MATERIALS

6 small cups
(for each taster)

Small bowls and
spoons

Appropriate
balsamics and
accompaniments

# LEARN YOUR
# PALATE

‧1‧ Swirl the vinegar against the cup's walls. To gauge its density, observe the coating that remains—vinegars aged for shorter periods of time will be more fluid, while those aged for longer will be more syrupy. (Excessiveness either way can reveal a defect.) Next, consider the color (color varies depending on grape variety, as well as cooking and aging methods).

‧2‧ Swirl the vinegar again, then bring your cup up to your nose and inhale deeply. What scents are you experiencing? Keep in mind that balsamics aged for shorter periods of time will smell more acidic, while those aged for longer will have sweeter and more complex aromas.

‧3‧ Now, sip a tiny bit of the vinegar and swirl it all over the inside of your mouth. What flavors are you experiencing? Are they mild or strong, spicy or sweet? How acidic is the vinegar? High-quality products should taste balanced—not jarring.

‧4‧ Describe the mouthfeel or texture. Is the vinegar thin and watery or thick and syrupy? After first trying the vinegar alone, experience it with the appropriate accompaniments (dip bread or cheese into the vinegar or drizzle the vinegar over strawberries or ice cream), then taste it again.

‧5‧ Do you like the sample? Would you purchase it?

# TASTING GRID

As you taste each sample, ask yourself the questions on the previous page and write your answers on a copy of this grid. Feel free to use the tasting terms provided below, and keep this grid for your future purchases.

| | ·1· | ·2· | ·3· | ·4· | ·5· | ·6· |
|---|---|---|---|---|---|---|
| **BALSAMIC VINEGAR NAME** | | | | | | |
| **APPEARANCE** *Density: thin and fluid versus syrupy and thick. Color: amber to dark or very dark brown.* | | | | | | |
| **AROMA** *Acidic, sweet, complex, wood, grapes, vanilla, cherry, cinnamon, clove, nutmeg, pleasant, unpleasant.* | | | | | | |
| **FLAVOR** *Mild, strong, spicy, sweet, acidic, complex, vanilla, cherry.* | | | | | | |
| **TEXTURE** *Thin and watery, thick and syrupy.* | | | | | | |
| **DO YOU LIKE IT?** | | | | | | |

# BALSAMIC VINEGAR
## *glossary*

**Acetaia:** Light, airy attics, where Tradizionale balsamic vinegar is aged in barrels.

**Acetify:** To turn into acetic acid or vinegar.

**Aceto:** Italian for vinegar.

**Batteria:** Series of barrels of different sizes and woods, in which Tradizionale balsamic vinegars age.

**Consorzio:** Consortium that oversees the quality of balsamic vinegar; two exist for Tradizionale.

**Emilia-Romagna:** Northern Italian region where balsamic vinegar originated; also where Aceto Balsamico Tradizionale is produced.

**Modena:** Province in the Northern Italian region of Emilia-Romagna

**Must:** Unfermented grape juice.

**Reggio-Emilia:** Province in the Northern Italian region of Emilia-Romagna.

**Trebbiano:** One of the several grape varieties used for Tradizionale.

**Vecchio (and Extravecchio):** Italian for "old" (and "very old"); designations for Tradizionale balsamic vinegar. The first generally refers to a product aged at least 12 years, while the second refers to a product aged 25 years or more.

# APPLES

*chapter ten*

Apples are inextricably bound with autumn—its symphony of falling leaves; crisp, wood smoke-tinged air; and the first hint of the heavy winter meals to come. Yet, since ancient times, they have also symbolized romance, healing, knowledge, and immortality.

Not bad for a fruit that seems almost pedestrian to the majority of us. With apple's availability year-round, it's the default fruit—common as an onion—rather than an eagerly anticipated treat. And that's a shame. To better appreciate this frequent denizen of our fruit bowl, why not have an apple tasting?

Since you'll want to gather apples at their peak, try to have this tasting in the fall. If you can, shop at a farmstand or farmer's market. Generally, they offer the most unusual, fresh apples, and you will have the opportunity to meet the folks behind the fruit.

# KNOW YOUR
# APPLES

It's not surprising that, with 10,000 varieties (according to one expert's count), apples range from petite to large, and squat to oblong. Their skins can be a myriad of colors, among them gold, green, pink, russet (reddish-brown), crimson, and deep purple. Some apples are soft and crumbly, while others are crisp and firm. Their flavor can be acidic, sweet, or complex, sometimes even evoking wine (Winesap), strawberries (Worcester Pearmain), and bananas (the Winter Banana).

Apples are further distinguished from one another by the time of year at which they ripen. The earliest fruits, including Arthur Turner, Melba, and Miller's Seedling, are generally soft and ready to be picked in the summer (usually July to August); they don't keep for long and are easily bruised. The next batch, including McIntosh, Arlet, and Ginger Gold, is a bit firmer and ripens in the early fall, keeping for several weeks. The final batch, called "late" or "winter," includes the firmest apples of all, which can be stored for six to eight months. These fruits, among them Dumelow's Seedling, Api (Lady Apple), and D'Arcy Spice, are picked before they're fully ripe, allowing them to develop their flavors while in storage.

Other than differentiating among early, mid-season, and late (or winter) apples, some experts classify the fruits by their most common usage: cooking, baking, or eating out of hand (known as "dessert"). The majority, though, fit in more than one category.

Cooking apples, such as Newtown Pippin, Bramley's Seedling, Golden Noble, Warner's King, and Dumelow's Seedling, are tart and soft, breaking down when exposed to heat (making them perfect for applesauce). Those best for baking, such as Rome Beauty, Jonathan, Golden Reinette, Blenheim Orange, and Golden Pippin, retain their shape at high heat. Eating apples, on the other hand, are sweet and sometimes highly complex in flavor; examples include Cox's Orange Pippin (thought to be one of the best varieties of eating apples in the world), Fuji, Gala, Mutsu (Crispin), Jonathan, Empire, Red Delicious, Ginger Gold, McIntosh, Braeburn, and Pink Lady.

> " Even if I knew that tomorrow the world would go to pieces, I would still plant my apple tree. "
>
> — Martin Luther King, Jr. (Baptist minister and political activist, 1929–1968)

## The Birds and the Bees . . . and Apples

Regardless of their characteristics, all apples in nature form in the same way: In the spring, apple trees blossom, and the male parts of their flowers produce pollen. When bees and butterflies visit these blossoms, they transfer this pollen to the female parts of blossoms on different trees. The female parts of these "fertilized" flowers turn into apple seeds, with the actual apples growing around them.

Since an apple blossom can only be fertilized by pollen from a different type of apple tree, the variety of the resulting seed is never exactly the same as the apple tree on which the blossom grew. In fact, the variety of the seed and resulting tree is a mystery—that is, until the tree grows and bears fruit.

Chance can be extremely generous: apple varieties that have been "discovered" as chance seedlings include (Red) Delicious, Golden Delicious, McIntosh, Granny Smith, Rome Beauty, and York Imperial.

## Grafting, Cross-Breeding, and More

Although variety and surprise are all well and good, growers generally want control over the varieties of trees they cultivate.

Thus, from ancient Rome to modern times, orchardists have, for the most part, eschewed the randomness of nature in favor of *grafting* (or budding). This is done in the spring, in two ways. In the first, a *scion* (a twig containing buds from the desired variety of tree) is inserted into a cleft of *rootstock* (a small, young tree). In the second method, growers remove a piece from rootstock and patch it with a piece of bud-containing bark from the desired variety of tree. Either way, the altered rootstock is protected in a nursery for up to two years before it's replanted.

The root of the expression, "an apple a day keeps the doctor away," is a medieval English saying: "Ate an apfel avore gwain to bed, make the doctor beg his bread."

Human interference doesn't end with cultivating pre-existing varieties, however. For the past couple of centuries, agricultural groups, such as the New York State Agricultural Experiment Station, have been developing new apple varieties, including the Macoun (from Mcintosh and Jersey Black), the Fuji (from Red Delicious and Ralls Janet), and the Jonagold (from Jonathan and Golden Delicious). To do this, they collect pollen from one cultivar and place it on the *stigma* ("female parts") of another. At the end of the season, the resulting fruit is collected and its seeds are extracted and sown, to produce seedlings. Since it can take up to ten years for seedlings to mature and bear fruit, scientists now often grow them for one to two years and then graft their buds onto rootstock. This way, the fruits come into being much sooner.

Along with creating new apple breeds, agricultural groups recommend varieties best suited to profitable farming—easy-to-grow, hardy apples that can be stored for long periods of time. This means that highly flavorful apples that happen to bruise easily, for example, have gone by the wayside, while unfussy, reliable varieties (such as Golden Delicious, Granny Smith, and McIntosh) have become more ubiquitous than ever. Thus, today, only about 13 to 15 apple varieties are grown and sold in large quantities.

To combat the prevalence of homogenous produce, a grassroots movement has sprung up to salvage "heirloom" or old breeds of apples. At the same time, in response to the growing demand for organic produce, growers have been trying to spray their apple trees less frequently (a difficult feat, since apple trees are highly susceptible to insects and disease). The odds are that you've seen some organic apples and perhaps a few heirloom varieties at your nearest gourmet grocery store, farmstand, or farmer's market.

## STORING APPLES

If you refrigerate apples, they can last for 90 days or more. Just make sure to handle them carefully (as they can bruise) and to store them away from foods with strong odors.

## THE LONG SHELF-LIFE OF APPLES

The main reason why apples are available year-round is cold storage technology, of which there are two types: basic cold storage (for short-term preservation) and the more costly controlled atmosphere storage, or CAS (for long-term holding). With the former, apples are picked when firm and stored in a humid 32°F environment. The cold air retards ripening (and spoilage), while the humidity prevents the apples from drying out.

In controlled atmosphere storage—invented in 1940 by Dr. Robert Smock of Cornell University—oxygen levels in airtight, humid warehouses are reduced to 2.5% (from 21%) with carbon dioxide levels increased to 2–5% (from 0.25%). Since oxygen causes apples to ripen and spoil, decreasing its presence dramatically hinders the ripening process.

| · VARIETY · | · ORIGIN · | · CHARACTERISTICS · |
|---|---|---|
| Braeburn | 1950s in New Zealand; unintentional cross-breed; believed to be Lady Hamilton seedling | Multipurpose; crisp, firm, juicy, sweet, and a bit spicy |
| Cortland | 1890s in New York (USA) | Multipurpose; sweet, a bit tart, soft, white flesh |
| Cox's Orange Pippin | 1825 in England; one parent believed to be Ribston Pippin | Complex, aromatic, with sweet, juicy, spicy, tender flesh |
| Egremont Russet | 1872 in England | Firm flesh, rich, nutty flavor |
| Empire | 1945 in New York (USA); intentional cross of Red Delicious and McIntosh | Multipurpose; crisp, juicy, sweet, and a bit tart |
| Fuji | 1939 in Japan; intentional cross of Ralls Janet and Delicious | Multipurpose; honey-sweet, firm |
| Gala | 1934 in New Zealand; cross of Golden Delicious and Kidd's Orange Red | Multipurpose; crisp, juicy, very sweet |
| Granny Smith | 1868 in Australia; one parent might be a French Crab apple | Multipurpose; firm, tart, acidic |
| Gravenstein | 1600s in Europe | Multipurpose; crisp and juicy |
| Honeycrisp | 1960 in Minnesota (USA); intentional cross of Macoun and Honeygold | Very crisp and juicy, slightly acidic |
| Idared | 1942 in Idaho (USA); intentional cross of Jonathan and Wagener | Multipurpose; tangy, crisp |
| Jonagold | 1968 in New York (USA); intentional cross of Jonathan and Golden Delicious | Multipurpose; crisp, juicy, honey-sweet and tart flesh |
| Macoun | 1923 in New York (USA); intentional cross of McIntosh and Jersey Black | Multipurpose; sweet, aromatic, juicy, strawberry flavor, tender white flesh |
| McIntosh | 1811 in Ontario (Canada); believed to come from a Fameuse or Saint Lawrence seedling | Multipurpose (although not good for baking); juicy, tangy, strawberry-flavored soft white flesh |
| Rhode Island Greening | Early 1700s in Rhode Island (USA) | Multipurpose; sweet, flavorful, juicy |
| Spartan | 1926 in British Columbia (Canada); cross of McIntosh and Yellow Newtown Pippin | Strawberry and melon flavor with some acidity |

*Note: This chart only includes a small variety of apples.*

# FIND YOUR
# APPLES

Your selection of apples will truly depend on your local supply. If you can, try to purchase varieties you've never before experienced. Also attempt to assemble a collection of fruits with different colors, flavors, and textures. And, remember: the next time you're overseas, sample as many apple varieties as you can. It's not easy to find a Cox's Orange Pippin in the United States (or a Rhode Island Greening in New Zealand, for that matter).

## SHOPPING FOR APPLES

To find the most delicious and interesting varieties, shop at your local farmstand, farmer's market, or orchard—you may even want to take a day trip to a more agricultural area. This way, you'll be able to learn from the source about the fruits you'll be tasting. As a bonus, in most cases, these apples won't wear sticky labels.

If you go to the grocery store instead, you'll likely find the same ten or so varieties that you've already tried. That's not necessarily a drawback, though, since you've probably never before savored apples in a structured fashion. In fact, you may find a tried-and-true tasting to be both fun and eye-opening.

Either way, make sure to choose firm, not dented, apples. Don't worry about "grades," which refer to color and size (and have nothing to do with flavor).

When shopping, remember to keep the various apple identities straight. Perhaps you could record the variety names on small slips of paper, and deposit them in the appropriate bags.

# CHOOSE YOUR
# ACCOMPANIMENTS

Begin your tasting with some Riesling or Gewürztraminer, as well as Cheddar with gingersnaps, and perhaps Chicken Apple Sausage in Puff Pastry with Cranberry-Golden Raisin Chutney (see page 215). As an alternative to the sausage, you can serve pigs in a blanket or other packaged hot hors d'oeuvres. With the apples, offer whole-wheat crackers and Buttered, Salted Pecans (see below). Consider finishing up the evening with some Port (a traditional accompaniment) or pecan tarts, blondies, oatmeal cookies, caramel popcorn, or gingerbread. To up the apple ante a notch, prepare Baked Apples with Crystallized Ginger, Armagnac Cider Syrup, and Crème Fraîche (see recipe on page 217).

## BUTTERED, SALTED PECANS

Melt two tablespoons of unsalted butter in a small-to-medium skillet over medium heat. Once the butter has melted, add two heaping cups of pecans and ½ teapoon of salt, and toast, stirring occasionally, until aromatic, about four minutes. Serve warm or at room temperature. For some extra heat, add a pinch of cayenne along with the salt.

Apples—with their skins on—are an excellent source of fiber and a good source of antioxidants. With just 80 calories per serving, the fruits also help to maintain a healthy weight.

# MENU

## APPETIZER

RIESLING

CHICKEN APPLE SAUSAGE IN PUFF PASTRY
WITH CRANBERRY-GOLDEN RAISIN CHUTNEY

CHEDDAR WITH GINGERSNAPS

## TASTING

GREENING

EMPIRE

CORTLAND

IDARED

MACOUN

FUJI

## ACCOMPANIMENTS

*Buttered, Salted Pecans and Whole-Wheat Crackers*

## DESSERT

*Miniature Pecan Tarts and Caramel Popcorn*

# RECIPES FOR ACCOMPANIMENTS AND AFTER

The pastries below are decadent and full of fall flavors, while the applesauce and baked apples on the next two pages are perfect uses for apple leftovers—here's hoping that lots of fruit remains after your tasting.

## CHICKEN APPLE SAUSAGE IN PUFF PASTRY
## WITH CRANBERRY GOLDEN RAISIN CHUTNEY

### MAKES 16 PIECES

*For fun, place any dough scraps on a baking sheet, sprinkle with sugar, cinnamon, and a hint of salt, and bake at 375° F until puffed and cooked through, about 10 minutes.*

### FOR THE PASTRY

**•1•** Preheat the oven to 375°F. In a small bowl, beat the egg with 1 teaspoon water. Set aside.

**•2•** Drizzle the oil in a heavy, medium-large skillet. Place over high heat. When hot, add the sausages and brown, about 2 minutes on the first side and 1 on the second. Transfer to a plate and let cool for about 15 minutes.

**•3•** Meanwhile, melt the butter with the salt and sage leaves in a small skillet over medium-low heat, about 3–4 minutes. Once melted, remove from the heat and let sit for 15 minutes.

**•4•** Line a baking sheet with parchment paper. Lightly flour your counter. Unroll the puff-pastry dough onto the floured surface. With a pastry cutter or knife, cut into four equal-sized squares, then brush with the cooled sage butter.

**•5•** Place a cooled sausage at the top of each piece, and roll up tightly, cutting off any excess dough. With a knife, gently score the top of each pastry four times, then transfer to the lined baking sheet, seam-side down. Repeat with the remaining 3 sausages and dough squares. Refrigerate for 20 minutes.

**•6•** Remove from the refrigerator and brush the tops with the egg wash. Place in the oven and bake until golden brown and flaky, about 30 minutes. Slice each log into four pieces (on the score lines) and serve immediately with the Cranberry Golden Raisin Chutney (see next page for recipe).

For the pastry:

1 large egg

1 tablespoon vegetable oil

12 ounces (4 links) precooked chicken apple sausage

2 tablespoons unsalted butter

Pinch salt

3 fresh sage leaves

All-purpose flour

1 sheet (14 ounces) puff pastry, defrosted according to package directions

## FOR THE CHUTNEY

MAKES ABOUT 1¾ CUPS

- •1• Cut a square piece of cheesecloth, and place the first three ingredients in the center. Bundle up and tie with kitchen twine. Place all of the ingredients, including this spice sachet, in a heavy small-to-medium saucepan.

- •2• Simmer over medium-high heat for about 5 minutes, stirring occasionally, then lower the heat to medium and simmer for another 3–5 minutes, until the berries have popped and the mixture has formed a thick sauce. Remove the sachet and as many of the orange zest strips as you can. Cool.

9 black peppercorns

8 cloves

2 cinnamon sticks

I teaspoon finely diced (or grated) fresh ginger root

I 12-ounce bag fresh (or frozen) cranberries (about 3 cups)

Zest of ½ large orange, in strips (white pith removed)

2 tablespoons cider vinegar

⅔ cup plus 2 tablespoons light brown sugar

I tablespoon Grand Marnier liqueur (or orange juice, or water)

½ cup golden raisins

¼ teaspoon salt

## EASY HOMEMADE APPLESAUCE

MAKES ABOUT 3 CUPS

*If you have any leftover apples, whip up a batch of this delicious applesauce, which can be prepared up to 3 days ahead. This is a fun recipe to make with children. If you're purchasing apples specifically for applesauce, try a combination of soft fruits, such as the following: Empire, McIntosh, Macoun, and Cortland. Including more than one variety makes for a more interesting finished product.*

- •1• Place apple pieces, lemon juice, and cider in a heavy medium saucepan. Cover and cook over medium heat until the apples are very soft and little liquid remains, about 20 minutes. (If too much liquid still remains, uncover and continue cooking until most of it evaporates.) Turn off the heat and mash with a potato masher. Add the syrup, cinnamon, salt, zest, and cardamom or ginger. (As all apples differ, taste and adjust the amount of maple syrup, if necessary.) Serve warm, cool, or at room temperature.

10 cups 1-inch cubes peeled, cored apple (from about 9 soft apples)

3 tablespoons freshly squeezed, strained lemon juice

¼ cup apple cider

I tablespoon plus I teaspoon pure maple syrup

⅛ teaspoon ground cinnamon

⅛ teaspoon salt

I heaping tablespoon freshly grated lemon zest

⅛ teaspoon ground cardamom (for a Middle Eastern flavor) or ground ginger (for a more traditional note)

## BAKED APPLES WITH CRYSTALLIZED GINGER, ARMAGNAC CIDER SYRUP, AND CRÈME FRAÎCHE

SERVES 4

*If you can't find Rome Beauties, try Golden Delicious apples; in a pinch, top the baked apples with vanilla ice cream instead of crème fraîche.*

•1• Preheat the oven to 350°F. In a small to medium bowl, combine the ginger, nuts, raisins, currants, 1 tablespoon of the maple syrup, cinnamon, and salt.

•2• In the bottom of a glass baking dish, combine the cider, Armagnac, 1 tablespoon of maple syrup, and 1 tablespoon of the butter.

•3• Using a large melon baller or a teaspoon, create a 1½-inch-wide cavity at the stem end of one apple, spooning out all of the seeds (don't go all the way to the bottom, though). With a vegetable peeler, peel off the skin from the top third of the apple, right around the cavity. Using a sharp knife, cut a very thin slice off the bottom, so that the apple may stand upright in the baking dish. Do the same with the remaining 3 apples.

•4• Place all 4 apples on top of the cider liquid in the baking dish. Spoon the nut-fruit mixture into all four cavities. Drizzle the remaining 1 tablespoon of maple syrup on top of the apples, and dot with the remaining 2 tablespoons of butter.

•5• Place on the middle rack in the oven, and bake uncovered until tender, about 1 hour (use a skewer to test for doneness; you want the apples to be soft, but still retain their shape). Once the apples are baked, transfer to a plate and cover with foil. Strain the liquid from the baking dish into a small, heavy saucepan and turn the heat to high. Boil until reduced to a syrupy consistency, about 11–13 minutes (this process might take longer, depending on your burner strength).

•6• Place each apple in a serving bowl. Spoon the syrup over the fruit, and top with a dollop of crème fraîche.

1½ tablespoons finely chopped crystallized ginger

½ cup pecans, finely chopped

2 tablespoons golden raisins

2 tablespoons currants

3 tablespoons maple syrup, divided

¼ teaspoon ground cinnamon

¼ teaspoon salt

1½ cups apple cider, preferably unpasteurized

¼ cup Armagnac (Cognac or Grand Marnier are also delicious)

3 tablespoons unsalted butter, diced, divided

4 Rome Beauty apples

Crème fraîche

# ORGANIZE YOUR
# TASTING

Set out six bowls or dinner plates, each representing one variety of apple (for example, one bowl would hold three Fuji apples, another Macoun, and so forth). Label each bowl with the appropriate variety name. However, don't cut the apples up until the tasting, as you want to avoid browning.

For the same reason, slice one variety of apple at a time—use a paring knife or apple corer (I prefer the former). Also, be sure to leave one of each type of apple intact so that everyone can evaluate its appearance. Cut each fruit into eight slices, offering each taster two of each variety.

Try to conduct this tasting near the kitchen so that you can wash your hands in between slicing apples. To play up the seasonal theme, consider decorating your table with autumn leaves.

## What You'll Need

Before conducting the tasting, make sure to have on hand "The Basics" (see Chapter 1), as well as the materials listed at right. By discarding unwanted apple slices in the bucket or bowl, your guests can keep their plates uncluttered. Whole-wheat crackers help to cleanse the palate and are a delicious accompaniment to fresh, crisp apples.

MATERIALS

Paring knife or apple corer

Cutting board

Bucket or bowl
(for discarding unwanted apple slices)

Appropriate apples and accompaniments, including nuts or whole-wheat crackers

# LEARN YOUR
# PALATE

First try each apple alone, and then sample it with the crackers and nuts. To make your tasting even more decadent, serve Port along with the apples.

- •1• Pass around, look at, and feel the whole apple. Consider its size; shape; and skin color, patterning, and texture. Now examine a slice of apple and evaluate the color of its flesh.

- •2• Bite into a slice of apple and think about the flavors you're experiencing. Is the fruit acidic or very sweet, for instance?

- •3• How would you describe the texture of the flesh? Is it soft, crumbly, and mealy, or crisp and firm? Juicy or dry?

- •4• Finally, ask yourself whether or not you like the apple. Would you purchase it?

# TASTING GRID

As you taste each apple, ask yourself the questions on the previous page and write your answers on a copy of this grid. Feel free to use the tasting terms provided below, and keep the grid as a record for future purchases.

| | ·1· | ·2· | ·3· | ·4· | ·5· | ·6· |
|---|---|---|---|---|---|---|
| **APPLE NAME** | | | | | | |
| **APPEARANCE**<br>*Size: petite, large.*<br>*Shape: squat or flat,*<br>*round, oblong, ribbed,*<br>*flat-sided, crowned.*<br>*Skin and flesh color:*<br>*gold, yellow, green,*<br>*pink, crimson, purple.*<br>*Patterning: nonexistent,*<br>*flushed, striped, russeted,*<br>*dotted, color fields*<br>*Texture: dry or waxy,*<br>*smooth or bumpy.* | | | | | | |
| **FLAVOR**<br>*Acidic, sweet, bland,*<br>*nutty, spicy, complex,*<br>*flavorful, redolent of*<br>*raspberries, strawberries,*<br>*pineapples, wine, honey.* | | | | | | |
| **TEXTURE**<br>*Soft, crumbly, mealy,*<br>*crisp, firm, juicy, dry.* | | | | | | |
| **DO YOU LIKE IT?** | | | | | | |

# APPLE
*glossary*

**Basic Cold Storage:** Short-term storage of apples in cold warehouses.

**Cultivar:** Cultivated variety (in this case, of an apple tree).

**Controlled Atmosphere Storage:** Long-term storage of apples in airtight, low-oxygen, high carbon-dioxide warehouses.

**Dessert Apples:** Apples with good flavor, meant for eating out of hand.

**Grafting (also called budding):** "Fusing" parts from a desired variety of tree onto rootstock to result in a new tree of the desired variety.

**Rootstock:** A small, young tree with roots.

**Russet:** Reddish-brown, usually rough skin.

**Scion:** Twig containing buds (of the desired variety of tree), used in grafting.

**Seedling orchards:** Orchards grown from seeds, as opposed to grafting.

# BEER

*chapter eleven*

For one of the most popular beverages in the world, beer is surprisingly underrated—virtually immune from pretension. Perhaps it's a victim of its own success: after serving as an everyday drink for so long, beer is now firmly associated with relaxed socialization. It's hard to imagine a bar without beers on tap.

Despite its casual image, beer is far from humble; it's actually as varied and complex as wine. Beer can be bitter, acidic, mild, or almost molasses-sweet, evoking fruit (lemons, apples, bananas, oranges, plums, and peaches), spices (coriander and cloves), bread, herbs, and even bubblegum, chocolate, and coffee!

The diversity doesn't stop there: Beer can range in color from pale yellow to butterscotch to deep motor-oil black, and in alcohol content from about 2.5–15% (beer has, on average, less than half the alcohol content of wine). You won't be surprised, then, to learn that this drink is extremely versatile, serving as an aperitif, meal accompaniment, or digestif. Because beer is so misunderstood, a beer tasting is truly an enlightening experience.

# KNOW
# YOUR
# **BEER**

Archaeologists have discovered evidence that beer—in essence, fermented grain juice—was consumed at least 8,000 years ago in Mesopotamia (modern-day Iraq). Not surprisingly, the drink flourished, especially in relatively cold areas hospitable to the growth of beer's key ingredients: hops, a climbing plant; and grain, primarily barley. Since barley meal produces dry, crumbly bread, our resourceful ancestors discovered that it's best used in beverages.

Over the years, beer's influence spread, and it became a popular drink in much of Western Europe, including Germany, Austria, England, Scotland, Ireland, Belgium, and the Czech Republic. Today, it's brewed all over the world—don't be surprised if you encounter a stein of Australian, Chinese, Japanese, Canadian, Caribbean, or African brew!

Although most beer is produced in large-scale breweries, of late there's been a "craft" or "renaissance" beer movement: microbreweries and brewpubs have sprung up to make artisanal and old-style brews. While microbreweries sometimes grow into larger operations, called regional breweries, brewpubs are content to serve their beers at their in-house restaurants.

## WHAT'S IN BEER?

Despite the dizzying array of varieties and packaging, beer always consists of grain, water, and yeast—with hops added in the vast majority of cases. Grain, the heart of beer, most often takes the form of malted barley; however, wheat, oats, rye, corn, and rice are sometimes used. While malted barley is relatively sweet, wheat adds fruitiness and acidity, oats silkiness, rye spiciness, and corn and cooked rice lightness (the latter two are generally used only in inexpensive American and Japanese lagers).

Amazingly, water accounts for 90–95% of beer's volume, which explains why the beverage is so refreshing. Beer's alcohol content comes from yeast, which is usually added to the grain and water mixture in the form of a culture. Yeast feeds on the grain sugars, producing alcohol and carbon dioxide.

The small green cones from hops, a climbing, perennial plant, are almost always an ingredient in beer. In fact, for beer to be labeled as such in the United States, it *must* contain hops. Dried and sold to breweries in whole, plug, pellet, or oil/extract form, hops add a bitter, floral, herbal flavor and aroma, and help to preserve the brew. Their bitterness balances out the sweetness of malt—the more hops, the higher a beer's level of bitterness (beers with a lot of hops are often referred to as hoppy, extra-hopped, and well-hopped).

For additional flavor, breweries sometimes include sweeteners (such as refined or dark sugar, honey, or lactose), spices (such as coriander, cinnamon, or cloves), or even fruit.

## How is Beer Made?

It all starts with the malting of the grain, which is usually carried out by maltsters, rather than the breweries themselves. Along with contributing much of beer's flavor, malting activates enzymes in the barley, which transform the grain's starch and complex proteins into compounds that can be more easily consumed by the yeast during fermentation.

To become malt, grain must first be soaked for a day or two. This encourages the second stage: *germination*, or sprouting. This process is generally halted by drying the grain. For specialty malts, the grain is sometimes toasted or roasted, which adds character. The exact manner in which the drying and roasting are carried out results in several different types of malt, named after cities (such as Vienna or Munich), colors (such as pale or black), or flavors (such as chocolate or roasted barley). These malts largely determine the flavor and color of the resulting brew. For example, malted barley that is gently dried results in a cracker-like flavor, while malted barley that is roasted until it is black (but not burnt) lends a chocolatey flavor to stout (a type of ale). Often, brewers use several different types of malt to add complexity to their beers.

❧❧❧

In ancient Mesopotamia, beer served as a primary part of the diet (along with onions, fish, bread, and seed-seasoning). In ancient Egypt, beer was used as currency.

❧❧❧

At the brewery, the malted grains are ground in a mill and deposited into a vessel, called a *mash tun* or *tub*. Hot water is added, and the mixture, known as *mash*, is steeped for one to two hours. The sweet liquid resulting from this process is called *wort*.

Next, the wort is filtered and added to a kettle, where it's boiled for an hour or two with hops. Brewing encourages the absorption of flavor from the hops, kills micro-organisms, and concentrates the liquid. Sometimes, one batch of hops is added at the beginning, to lend bitterness, another in the middle to pick up hops flavor, and a final towards the end, to impart hops aroma.

At this point, the unfermented beer is strained, cooled down, and transferred to fermentation vessels, where yeast is added. During this process, the yeast feeds on the sugar-rich wort, producing alcohol and carbon dioxide. Some types of beer, usually lager, are moved to conditioning tanks, where they mature—occasionally, hops are added to the fermentation or conditioning tanks to lend additional flavor, a process known as dry-hopping. From the conditioning tanks, the beer progresses to bottles, kegs, or cans.

Finally, some beers are carbonated before bottling. For bottle-conditioned brews, though, actively fermenting beer or a combination of yeast and sugar is added to the entire batch of beer instead. Alternatively, beer is bottled before the fermentation process has ended, meaning that carbon dioxide is generated and released within the bottle's walls.

## 300 Bottles of Beer on the Wall

In 1516, a German beer purity law, *Reinheitsgebot*, ruled that beer could only consist of malted barley or wheat, yeast (often brewers yeast, or *Saccharomyces cerevisiae*), water, and hops; sugar, rice, corn, unmalted barley, or chemicals could not be used. Today, many beers diverge from this formula. In fact, beer is far from homogenous— a myriad of types and recipes exist. Although beer can be classified in several ways, there is an easy-to-follow system for understanding the different types.

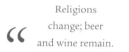

Religions change; beer and wine remain.

—Hervey Allen
(American novelist and poet, 1889–1949)

Top-fermented beers, known as *ales*, are made with yeast that rises to the surface during brewing. This yeast prefers environments of around 65–75°F; fermentation and maturation periods are only about seven to ten days. The ale family, considered fruity, includes pale, bitter, English brown, Scottish, and Trappist ales, as well as *porters* and *stouts*—the latter of which are sometimes placed in their own category. These very dark brews frequently taste of roasted nuts, espresso, or chocolate.

Bottom-fermented brews, known as *lagers* (*lagern* means "to store" in German), are made with yeast that sinks to the bottom during fermentation. This yeast prefers environments of around 32–48°F, resulting in fermentation and maturation periods that are longer than for ale.

Lagers were invented by Bavarian monks during the Middle Ages. Due to high bacteriological activity resulting from heat, brewing during the summer generally would have soured the beer. As a result, the monks discovered that storing the year's last batch of brew in icy caves during the warmer months preserved the beers and resulted in mellow, rounded flavors. Furthermore, because cold storage retarded spoilage, the monks could use lower levels of alcohol and hops (both preservatives). This meant that the resulting lager could be consumed in larger quantities, with broader appeal. Today, lagers are fermented and aged in refrigerated rooms, and have become the most popular beer style in many countries, including the United Kingdom, the United States, the Czech Republic, and Germany. Just think of the prevalence of pilsner and its many derivatives, including "light" beer.

*Wheat beers*, made with at least 50% wheat, are another category. While most are fermented with basic ale yeast, Bavarian-style wheat beer involves what is known as *weizen, weisse,* or *weiss* (German for "white") yeast. Weizen yeast is actually top-fermenting; however, it's so different genetically from ale yeast that it's given its own category. This yeast lends this style of beer (also known as *Weizen*) its banana, clove, and vanilla flavors. All styles of wheat beer are light, refreshing, and somewhat acidic. Wheat beer is often fruity, carbonated, and low-alcohol as well.

Outside of these categories, some beers are made with lager yeasts, yet are fermented and aged at ale temperatures; these are considered *combination* specimens. For smoked beer, the grain is dried over wood fires, while rye beer is made with rye as well as barley. For fruit beers, fruit, fruit syrup, or fruit flavoring is added, usually during fermentation. This provides flavor and adds sugars on which the yeast feeds. Finally, *seasonal* or *holiday brews* are made at specific times of the year; the latter

The bitterness of beer is measured in International Bitterness Units (IBUs).

usually includes spices, such as cloves. Within each of these categories, you'll find many classes of beer. The chart on the opposite page
will help you begin to keep them straight.

## A FEW TYPES OF BEER

*Michael Jackson's Beer Companion*
proved invaluable in compiling
this chart; I largely borrowed the
categorization system from him.
Keep in mind that beers can be
placed in more than one category;
for example, many wheat beers and
most porters and stouts are ales.

Although many of the beer
styles or types below are associated with specific countries or areas,
breweries all over the world produce
imitations. Thus, a brewery in Kenya
can make Belgian-style wheat ale.

As mentioned previously, some
beers, such as fruit or spice, can be
lumped under an "Other" category.
Another example is California
Common California Common,
Dampfbier, or Steam beer (the latter
name is copyrighted by California's
Anchor Brewing Company). This is a
hoppy, amber brew made with lager
yeasts fermented in shallow vessels at
warm temperatures.

## Classified BEER KEY

❋ **TOP-FERMENTED OR ALE**
The yeasts for these fruity, age-old beers rise
to the surface during brewing. The British call
ale "beer" to differentiate it from lager.

▨ **PORTER AND STOUT**
Very dark and opaque, both types of brew
are usually top-fermented and made with
toasted and roasted malts. Porters are a lighter
derivative of stouts.

▦ **BOTTOM-FERMENTED OR LAGER**
For the most part, lagers make up the majority
of everyday beers throughout the world. The
resulting brew is dry, light, clear, carbonated,
low-alcohol, and refreshing. "Light" refers
to brews that are low in alcohol, calories,
and often, flavor.

❅ **LAMBIC**
Lambics are cloudy yellow, somewhat acidic
wheat beers, made with wild yeasts and
bacteria.

※ **WHEAT OR WHITE BEER**
Wheat beers are made with a substantial
percentage of wheat; many are bottle-
fermented and cloudy from yeasts and protein.
You'll find these brews to be carbonated, tart,
low-alcohol, light, and refreshing.

| · TYPE · | · CHARACTERISTICS · |
|---|---|
| ❋ Bitter | Bitter; primary ale style sold in Britain, as Ordinary, Best, or Extra Special Bitter (ESB), depending on strength |
| ❋ Pale | Bitter, slightly nutty; a subcategory, India Pale Ale (IPA) is very bitter and dry, and fairly alcoholic |
| ❋ English Brown | Originally dark and sweet; now, slightly bitter |
| ❋ Barley Wine | Most alcoholic of all ales; dark, sweet, heavy; long-fermented and –matured |
| ❋ Flemish or Flanders Brown | Complex, acidic, refreshing, sometimes sweet, reddish-brown; occasionally a blend of young and old beers |
| ❋ Trappist and Abbey (or Klosterbier if German Abbey-Style) | Trappist ales are produced by one of the following six monasteries (the first five are Belgian and the sixth is Dutch): Chimay, Orval, Rochefort, Westmalle, Westvleteren (or St. Sixtus), and Schaapskooi at Koningshoeven. All are bottle-conditioned, fairly alcoholic, and complex. Single, double, and triple indicates the strength of the brews. The designation "Abbey-style" can refer to beers made in the traditional abbey way or can just be used for marketing. |
| ❋ Altbier (or Düsseldorfer Alt) | Malty, bitter, copper-colored; sometimes considered a "combination" beer since it's lager-aged |
| ❋ American (Stock, Cream, Gold, Amber, or Western-style) | Stock: winey; Cream: mild, pale, sparkling, slightly sweet; Gold: fresh, somewhat fruity, made with light malt; Amber: usually indicates the color only, sometimes used for lagers, too; Western-style: pale, somewhat hoppy |
| ❋ Bière de Paris (or de Garde) (name means "beer to keep") | Often malty, spicy, fruity, somewhat alcoholic; bottle-conditioned, often in champagne bottles; some are lagers |
| ⌗ Porter | Often malty, sweet, spicy, chocolatey; some include chocolate malt, black malt, licorice root, and roasted barley |
| ⌗ Milk, English, Sweet, or European Stout | Very flavorful, usually reminiscent of coffee and chocolate, usually not high-alcohol, sweet (often from lactose, or milk sugar) |
| ⌗ Dry or Irish Stout | Well-hopped, coffee flavor, creamy; made with roasted unmalted or flaked barley |
| ⌗ Imperial, Baltic, or Russian Stout | Intense, highly alcoholic, dry and roasted flavor |
| ⌗ Vienna-Style/Marzen/Oktoberfest | Sweetish, spicy, somewhat strong; made with Vienna malt |
| ⌗ Pilsener (Pilsner, Pils) | World's palest lager and most widely made style; the "real thing" (imitations abound) is well-hopped, flowery, and dry; the American version, called "Premium Lager," is generally light, highly carbonated, and sometimes made with corn and rice |
| ⌗ Dark/Kulmbacher/Münchner Dunkel/Dunkles | Dark brown, spicy, malty, heavy (black brews are called "Schwartz," German for black) |
| ⌗ Golden Lager or Helles (or Hell) | Originally German, clear or light-colored |
| ⌗ Bock (can also apply to strong wheat beers, below) | Highly alcoholic, malty, and well-hopped, somewhat sweet, medium-to-dark color |
| ❋ Lambic | Tart, not carbonated, can be difficult to find |
| ❋ Gueuze | Somewhat sweet, acidic, sparkling; a blend of young and old lambics; bottle-fermented |
| ❋ Fruit Lambic | Dry and fruity; fruit (usually raspberries: frambozen/framboise; or cherries: kriek) added during fermentation |
| ※ Belgian-Style (Bière Blanche or Witbier) | Fruity, pale, sedimented; flavored with (bitter) orange peels, coriander seeds, and cumin (sometimes oats and ginger are used in the USA) |
| ※ Berlin-Style (Berliner Weiss) | Sour from the use of a lactic culture; sometimes served with a fruit or herb syrup |
| ※ Bavarian- or South German-Style (Weizen, Weiss, Weisse) | Experts describe these beers as having clove, apple, plum, banana, vanilla, and bubblegum notes; some undergo bottle-fermentation. Kristall Weizen refers to filtered brews (without bottle fermentation); Hefeweizen, Hefe-Weisse, and mit Hefe mean unfiltered, cloudy, bottle-conditioned brews. Strong, dark beers are referred to as Bocks (e.g., Weizenbock), Dunkel, or Dunkle (similar to dark lagers, above). |

# FIND
# YOUR
# **BEER**

I recommend first having an introductory tasting, where you include a sample in each of six categories, starting with a variety or style known to everyone. For example, consider beginning with a light lager, then progressing to a fruit lambic, a dark South German-style wheat beer, rye beer, Trappist ale, and finally stout. Whatever you decide, it's best to stick with products that are representative of their genre. For example, you might want to avoid a porter with hazelnut flavoring. Go for the traditional, so that you can experience canonical examples.

If you're a beer aficionado or have already participated in an introductory beer tasting, you can narrow your focus. Try a pure ale, lager, lambic, or even stout, fruit beer, or seasonal brew-tasting. Only try beers from Germany, Belgium, Britain, or the United States, or limit your tasting to beers made by microbreweries. For fun, you can even include one of the world's most expensive beers: Samuel Adams' Utopias, which comes in a copper bottle, has 25% alcohol, and costs $100 or more (I once came across a 2003 bottle on www.ebay.com for $289.99!).

## Shopping for Beer

Because everyone will taste about ⅓ cup of each sample, you'll need two 12-ounce bottles of each beer for every eight people. Try your local liquor and gourmet stores, or Internet sites, such as www.beergeek.biz, www.beerliquors.com, or www.internetwines. com/beer (keep in mind, though, that some states prohibit alcohol

shipments). Note that some beers, including Trappist ales, are packaged in larger bottles. Since beer volume is often expressed in liters, it may help to remember that one liter is equivalent to about five cups (or one quart, plus about one cup).

Hopefully, stores will let you purchase individual bottles. If not, don't worry—beer isn't too expensive. Just buy four- or six-packs and know that you'll have plenty of beer around for your next party. If you buy 12 bottles (a "case") or more, ask for a discount; many stores will take 10% off the purchase price. Online, you'll be able to purchase some bottles (often, larger ones) individually, or at least in 4-packs.

If you can, check packaging dates—generally, the fresher, the better. Also keep in mind that not all labeling is accurate; for instance, ale might be labeled as lager, and so forth. Always read the information on the label to learn as much as you can about the beer before purchasing.

As an alternative to shopping for your tasting, consider having your event at a bar or brewpub with an extensive beer menu—just make sure to ask the establishment in advance. That way, you'll have access to a wide variety of beer, and they'll take care of procuring the drinks, providing any food, and washing the dishes for you. I can't think of a better gift for a beer-lover!

# STORING & SERVING BEER

The vast majority of beers are meant to be consumed fresh, within six, but preferably three, months of bottling. However, you can try high-alcohol, highly hopped, bottle-conditioned beers (such as Trappist ales, porters, stouts, and barley wines) up to one year or more after packaging.

Store your beer at a cool temperature, and do your best to shield it from light. Generally, ales are served at 50–55°F, while lagers are served at 40–45°F. For a tasting, serve your beer at slightly warmer temperatures than these. That way, the beers' flavors and aromas will be more easily detectable. I recommend removing the bottles from the refrigerator 30 minutes to an hour before serving.

You may have noticed that different beers are served in different types of glasses. For example, barley wine is traditionally served in a cordial glass, pale ale in a dimpled pub mug, pilsner in a pilsner glass, Bavarian Helle or American lager in a tankard, Bavarian wheat beer in a weissbier tumbler, and so forth. Unless you're a bar—and a beer-centric one at that—you probably don't own this many beer glasses. If you do, this is the perfect time to use them. If not, try narrow, tall water glasses (which allow the formation of a head, or foam) or wine glasses (for strong beers, such as barley wine).

Whichever type of glasses you choose, make sure that they're squeaky clean, with no traces of dishwashing liquid or soap. If you like, you can refrigerate your glasses for about 30 minutes to one hour before the tasting (while you're letting your samples warm up).

Most beers should first be poured down the side of the glass, and then directed into the center of the vessel (pouring straight down from the get-go will yield too large a head).

# CHOOSE YOUR
## ACCOMPANIMENTS

Since you don't want to get tipsy prior to the tasting, begin with glasses of sparkling and still mineral water with slices of fresh fruit. Serve down-to-earth fare: Homemade Cheese Balls (see recipes on page 241) with crackers; assorted hot *wursts* (sausages) and Flavored Mustards (see recipes on page 242) or a large hero; and add a salad if your tasting is taking place around mealtime.

Although many would assume that salty, crunchy potato chips, pretzels, or nuts would pair best with beer, they're actually not ideal for a tasting; in fact, these foods would interfere with the subtle nuances of the beer. (Stick with them when you're not deep-tasting.) Instead, go with a more neutral accompaniment, such as plain bread or crackers. Finally, conclude the tasting with some fun sweets, such as Chocolate-Covered Pretzels and Strawberries (see recipe on page 243), or stick with crowd-pleasers like chocolate cake, vanilla-scented pound cake, or even gingerbread.

Alternatively, plan your menu around traditional beer accompaniments. Epicures swear by serving fruit lambics as appetite-inducers, stout with oysters, Pilsner with rich cream soups, and barley wines as night-caps.

> " Without question, the greatest invention in the history of mankind is beer. Oh, I grant you that the wheel was also a fine invention, but the wheel does not go nearly as well with pizza. "
>
> —Dave Barry
> (Writer, 1947– )

# MENU

## APPETIZER

SPARKLING AND STILL MINERAL WATER WITH CITRUS SLICES

HOMEMADE CHEESE BALLS WITH CRACKERS

ASSORTED HOT SAUSAGES WITH FLAVORED MUSTARDS

BITTER GREENS SALAD WITH TANGERINES, TOASTED
ALMONDS, AND RASPBERRY VINAIGRETTE

## TASTING

PILSENER *(Try a Czech product—they invented this type of beer in the first place)*

FRUIT LAMBIC OR GUEUZE *(The "real thing" is always Belgian)*

WEIZENBIER MIT HEFE *(South German-Style Wheat Beer, with yeast)*

STEAM BEER *(I would try the American original, Anchor Steam)*

TRAPPIST ALE *(These are Belgian or, in one case, Dutch)*

MILK OR OATMEAL STOUT *(Try a British product)*

## ACCOMPANIMENT

*Plain crackers*

## DESSERT

*Chocolate-Covered Pretzels and Strawberries*

# RECIPES FOR ACCOMPANIMENTS

The salt in the cheese balls and the pungent mustards will spur on thirst, while the beer will echo the bitter and sweet flavors in the salad. Chocolate-covered pretzels and strawberries are a fun, casual way to end the tasting.

## HOMEMADE PORT AND CHEDDAR BALL WITH TOASTED PECANS

MAKES 1 BALL

*If you'd prefer an orange color, purchase Cheddar or Colby with an orange hue. The cheese ball will be slightly difficult to work with, but will hold together after being chilled for an hour.*

•1• Using the large holes of a box grater, grate the cheese into a medium-sized bowl. Add the Port, mustard, and pepper and mix with your hands. Shape into a ball.

•2• Place the nuts on a medium-sized piece of aluminum foil. Roll the cheese ball in the nuts, coating its entire surface. Press in any remaining nuts with your hands. Wrap the cheese ball in the foil and refrigerate for at least an hour. Remove from the fridge 30 minutes before serving. (The cheese ball can be prepared one day in advance.)

8 ounces Cheddar cheese

3 tablespoons ruby Port

¼ teaspoon Dijon mustard

¼ cup pecans or walnuts, toasted and finely chopped

4 grinds black pepper

## HOMEMADE GORGONZOLA BALL WITH PISTACHIOS AND DRIED CHERRIES

MAKES 1 BALL

*Remove the cheese from the refrigerator about one hour before preparing this recipe.*

•1• In a medium-sized bowl, combine the softened cheese, chives, pepper, and cherries. Using your hands, shape into a ball.

•2• Place the nuts on a medium-sized piece of aluminum foil. Roll the cheese ball in the nuts, coating its entire surface. Press in any remaining nuts with your hands. Wrap the cheese ball in the foil and refrigerate for at least 30 minutes. Remove from the fridge 30 minutes before serving. (The cheese ball can be prepared one day in advance.)

10 ounces soft blue cheese, such as Gorgonzola Dolce or Maytag Blue

1 tablespoon minced fresh chives

4 grinds black pepper

¼ cup dried cherries, finely chopped

¼ cup shelled pistachios, toasted and finely chopped

## FLAVORED MUSTARDS

MAKES ½ CUP EACH

*It's fun to serve hot sausages with a variety of flavored mustards. Why not make them yourself? It's easy: for each variety, just measure ½ cup of smooth, unflavored Dijon mustard into a small bowl. Then add the following ingredients.*

### RASPBERRY

Stir in 2 tablespoons plus 1 teaspoon raspberry jam. Alternatively, try apricot jam.

### PAPRIKA

Stir in 1 teaspoon paprika.

### CAPER

Stir in 6 tablespoons drained, rinsed, brine-packed capers. Alternatively, try chopped cornichons.

## BITTER GREENS SALAD WITH ORANGES, TOASTED ALMONDS, AND RASPBERRY VINAIGRETTE

SERVES 8

*The bitterness of the greens contrasts with the sweetness of the oranges. The toasted almonds add a bit of crunch.*

•1• If using endive and radicchio, thinly slice. Wash the greens thoroughly in cold water, dry (preferably in a salad spinner), and chill. (My method is, after drying, to place a few dry paper towels on top of the greens and to place the entire salad spinner in the refrigerator until I'm ready to dress and serve the salad.)

•2• When ready to serve, add the greens to a large bowl. Sprinkle with salt and pepper. Add half of the vinaigrette and gently toss. With tongs, divide the salad among eight plates. Top each portion with some orange segments and toasted almonds, drizzle with the remaining vinaigrette, and serve.

8 cups bitter greens, including endive, radicchio, or arugula

1 teaspoon coarse salt and 6 grinds black pepper to taste

¾ cup homemade or store-bought raspberry vinaigrette, divided

6 large navel oranges, peeled, thinly sliced into rounds, and rounds halved

½ cup slivered almonds, lightly toasted

# CHOCOLATE-COVERED PRETZELS AND STRAWBERRIES

MAKES 28 STRAWBERRIES AND 50 PRETZELS

*It's best to prepare the strawberries right before your guests arrive—they can "sweat" in the refrigerator. If you decide to make the pretzels in advance, gently place them on layers of wax paper in airtight containers and store at room temperature for up to five days. If you have leftover chocolate, spoon it out of the bowl as is or make* mendiants *(you should be able to form 8 that are 1½ inches in diameter): Onto a piece of wax paper, spoon circles of chocolate. Sprinkle with nuts, coconut, or small pieces of dried fruit. Let set and enjoy!*

•1• Wash the strawberries and dry very well (don't hull them). Make sure that all of the berries are fresh and attractive. Place both the pretzels and berries next to your range.

•2• Set the two types of nuts and the coconut in separate piles on a cutting board and also place alongside your range. Line three baking sheets with wax or parchment paper and set there as well.

•3• Fill a medium pot a quarter full of water and bring to a steady simmer over low-medium heat. Place the chopped chocolate in a medium-sized stainless steel bowl and set the bowl over the pot. Stir frequently as the chocolate melts, about 2 minutes.

•4• Once the chocolate has melted, turn off the heat (but leave the bowl on top of the pot). Dip the pretzels so that they're covered in chocolate about ⅔ of the way up. Use a spoon to help you cover each side with the chocolate. Shake off any excess chocolate, and, if you like, over the cutting board, sprinkle every chocolate-covered surface with one of the toppings. Place each finished pretzel on the wax paper, and repeat with the strawberries (lift the berries by their leaves).

•5• Let both the pretzels and strawberries sit at room temperature until they've set, about 45 minutes (you'll know they're done when the chocolate no longer looks wet and shiny and can be removed from the wax paper without sticking). Serve the berries immediately.

I pound strawberries
(about 28 berries)

50 pretzel sticks
(2 inches long by
I inch wide)

¼ cup toasted
shelled pistachios,
finely chopped

¼ cup toasted slivered
(blanched) almonds,
finely chopped

¼ cup sweetened
shredded coconut

10 ounces sweetened
chocolate (I like bars
with 71% cocoa),
coarsely chopped

# ORGANIZE YOUR
# TASTING

Make sure to consult the chart on page 233 to determine the characteristics each style of beer should have; this way, you will know how to judge whether the samples are true to their style.

## WHAT YOU'LL NEED

Before conducting the tasting, make sure to have on hand "The Basics" (see Chapter 1), as well as the materials below. Remove the bottles from the refrigerator about 30 minutes to 1 hour before the tasting. Arrange them in order from mildest to strongest (the same order in which you'll taste them). Wait until the tasting to open the bottles—and open them one at a time to prevent the later beers from going flat before you taste them.

Pour about ⅓ cup of each beer for each taster. There's no need to rinse glasses between beers, but you can discard any unwanted beer in the bucket on the table. Remember to cleanse your palate with the bread or crackers and water.

If you're tasting a cloudy brew (like a wheat beer), you might want to swish around the liquid at the bottom of your glass to integrate any sediment thoroughly.

### MATERIALS

Bottle opener

Beer or tall glasses—
one per guest

Bucket or bowl
(for discarding
unwanted beer)

Appropriate beers

Plain bread (such as
baguettes or ciabatta)
or unsalted, mild,
white-flour crackers

# LEARN YOUR
# PALATE

•1• Study the beer. Describe its head (foam), color, and level of clarity. "Lace" is a term for head that sticks to the sides of the glass and resembles its namesake—does this beer form lace? Contrary to common belief, a darker color does not always mean a stronger, more flavorful brew. If the beer is cloudy, there's a good chance that it wasn't filtered, and, thus, still contains some yeast. Wheat beers are generally cloudy, as a result of proteins and yeast. Keep in mind that carbonation shouldn't factor into your evaluation of the beer's clarity.

•2• Now, swirl the glass and bring it up to your nose. Close your eyes and inhale. What aromas do you detect?

•3• Swirl the glass again and take a sip, distributing the beer all around the inside of your mouth. What flavors are you experiencing? Swallow the beer (doing so is necessary to gauge its full bitterness) and consider its finish (or aftertaste). Is it long or short, meaning do the flavors dissipate quickly or last for a while in your mouth? What flavors remain?

•4• Take another sip and consider the body of the beer. Is it thick and velvety or light and thin?

•5• Referring to the chart on page 233, determine whether this beer is true to its style.

•6• Finally, ask yourself whether you like it.

# TASTING GRID

As you taste each beer, ask yourself the questions on the previous page and write your answers on a copy of this grid. Feel free to use the tasting terms provided below, and keep a copy of this for future beer purchases.

| | ·1· | ·2· | ·3· | ·4· | ·5· | ·6· |
|---|---|---|---|---|---|---|
| **BEER NAME** | | | | | | |
| **APPEARANCE** *Head: size, size of bubbles, lace. Color: pale gold, honey, amber, butterscotch, mahogany, dark brown, black. Clarity: clear or cloudy.* | | | | | | |
| **AROMA** *Strong or mild, peaches, lemons, tart, herbal, nutty, bread, molasses, coffee, chocolate, burnt.* | | | | | | |
| **FLAVOR AND FINISH** *Flavor: strong or mild, bitter, acidic, sweet, peaches, plums, lemons, apples, oranges, coriander, cloves, nuts, bread, molasses, coffee, chocolate. Finish: long or short, bitter, acidic, etc.* | | | | | | |
| **BODY** *Full or thin.* | | | | | | |
| **TRUE TO STYLE?** *Yes or no.* | | | | | | |
| **DO YOU LIKE IT?** | | | | | | |

# BEER

*glossary*

**ABV:** Alcohol by volume, the percentage of the beer composed of alcohol (if you see ABW, know that it refers to alcohol by weight; ABW is 80% of ABV).

**Ale:** Top-fermented beer, in which the yeast rises to the surface during brewing; fermented and matured at fairly warm temperatures.

**Barley:** The primary grain from which beer is made.

**Bottle-Conditioned or -Conditioning:** Actively fermenting beer or a combination of sugar and yeast is added to the batch of beer before bottling; in the bottle, the beer continues to ferment (alternatively, beer is bottled before the fermentation process has ended).

**Hops:** A vining perennial plant, whose small green cones are dried and packaged in whole, plug, pellet, or oil/extract form. Used to preserve beer, as well as to add a flowery, herbal, bitter flavor. **Hoppy** or **well-hopped** refers to a bitter-tasting brew. **Dry-hopped** means that hops were added to the brew during fermentation or maturation.

**Lager:** Bottom-fermented beer, in which the yeast drops to the bottom of the liquid during fermentation; fermented and matured at fairly cold temperatures, for a longer period of time than ale.

**Lambic:** Belgian wheat beer fermented by wild yeast and bacteria.

**Malt:** Byproduct of cereal grains (usually barley) that have been soaked, dried, and then toasted or roasted; lends beer its color and much of its flavor.

**Wort:** Unfermented grain-infused water.

## WINE

*Great Wine Made Simple: Straight Talk from a Master Sommelier* by Andrea Immer Robinson (Broadway, September 2005)
*The Wall Street Journal Guide to Wine: New and Improved: How to Buy, Drink, and Enjoy Wine* by Dorothy J. Gaiter, John Brecher (Broadway, September 2002)
*Windows on the World Complete Wine Course: 2006 Edition* by Kevin Zraly (Sterling, September 2005)
*Wine Style: Earthy Whites to Powerful Reds: Using Your Senses to Explore and Enjoy Wine* by Mary Ewing-Mulligan, Ed McCarthy (Wiley, October 2005)
*Wine for Dummies* by Ed McCarthy, Mary Ewing-Mulligan (John Wiley & Sons, August 2003)
www.winespectator.com
www.wine.about.com

## CHOCOLATE

*The Everything Chocolate Cookbook: A Chocolate-Lover's Dream Collection of Cookies, Cakes, Brownies, Candies, and Confections* by Laura Tyler Samuels (Adams Media Corporation, November 2000)
*Indulgence: Around the World in Search of Chocolate* by Paul Richardson (Abacus, UK, April 2004)
*The New Taste of Chocolate: A Cultural and Natural History of Cacao with Recipes* by Maricel Presilla (Ten Speed Press, September 2001)
*New York Chocolate Lovers Guide: The Best Candy, Cakes and Chocolate Treats in Town* by William Gillen, Patricia MacKenzie (City and Company, November 1996)
www.worldcocoafoundation.org
www.cocoatree.org
www.icco.org
www.chocolateusa.org

## CHEESE

*Cheese: Selecting, Tasting, and Serving the World's Finest* by Alix Baboin-Jaubert (Laurel Glen Publishing, January 2003)
*The Cheese Course* by Janet Fletcher (Chronicle Books, July 2000)
*The Cheese Plate* by Max McCalman, David Gibbons (Clarkson Potter, March 2002)
*Cheese Primer* by Steven Jenkins (Workman Publishing Company, November 1996)
*Cheese: A Connoisseur's Guide to the World's Best* by Max McCalman, David Gibbons (Clarkson Potter, August 2005)
http://encyclopedia.laborlawtalk.com/List_of_cheeses
www.gourmetspot.com/factscheese.htm
www.cheese.com
www.cheesesociety.org
www.ilovecheese.com

## HONEY

*A Book of Honey* by Eva Crane (Oxford University Press, December 1980)
*Covered in Honey: The Amazing Flavors of Varietal Honey* by Mani Niall (Rodale Books, September 2003)
*Honey: From Flower to Table* by Stephanie Rosenbaum, Caroline Kopp (photographer) (Chronicle Books, March 2002)
www.nhb.org
www.honey.com
www.honeyassociation.com

## TEA

*Eat Tea: Savory and Sweet Dishes Flavored with the World's Most Versatile Ingredient* by Joanna Pruess, John Harney (The Lyons Press, December 2001)
*Pleasures of Tea: Recipes & Rituals* by Kim Waller (Hearst, December 2001)
*Serendipitea: A Guide to the Varieties, Origins, and Rituals of Tea* by Tomislav Podreka (William Morrow & Company, September 1998)
*Tea: Essence of the Leaf* by Karl Petzke, Linda Berry, Sara Slavin, Lesley Berry (Chronicle Books, April 1998)
*The Tea Lover's Companion: The Ultimate Connoisseur's Guide to Buying, Brewing, and Enjoying Tea* by James Norwood Pratt, Diana Rosen (Carol Publishing Corporation, February 1996)
www.teausa.org
www.teasociety.org
http://en.wikipedia.org/wiki/tea

## EXTRA VIRGIN OLIVE OIL

*The Flavors of Olive Oil: A Tasting Guide and Cookbook* by Deborah Krasner (Simon & Schuster, September 2002)
*Olive Oil: From Tree to Table* by Peggy Knickerbocker (Chronicle Books, October 1997)
www.worldpantry.com
www.delizia.com

www.williams-sonoma.com
www.waitrose.com
www.cooc.com
www.internationaloliveoil.org
http://aboutoliveoil.org
www.oliveoilsource.com
www.oliveoil.gr
www.evoliveoil.com

## CURED MEATS

*Bruce Aidells's Complete Book of Pork: A Guide to Buying, Storing, and Cooking the World's Favorite Meat* by Bruce Aidells (Morrow, November 2004)
*The Great Book of Sausages* by Antony Hippisley Coxe, Araminta Hippisley Coxe (Overlook TP, October 1996)
*Making Great Sausage at Home: 30 Savory Links from Around the World—Plus Dozens of Delicious Sausage Dishes* by Chris Kobler (Lark Books, March 2002)
*Salt: A World History* by Mark Kurlansky (Walker & Company, January 2002)
*Food & Wine Magazine*, "A Party Cure-All," by Ray Isle, January 2006
www.academiabarilla.com
www.rusticocooking.com
www.salumicuredmeats.com
http://italianfood.about.com
www.hot-dog.org
www.sausagefans.com

## BALSAMIC VINEGAR

*Balsamico!: A Balsamic Vinegar Cookbook* by Pamela Sheldon Johns (Ten Speed Press, February 1999)
www.academiabarilla.com
www.balsamico.it
www.consorziobalsamico.it
www.aib-online.org

## APPLES

*All About Apples* by Alice A. Martin (Houghton Mifflin, January 1976)
*Apples: A Country Garden Cookbook* by Christopher Idone, Kathryn Kleinman (Photographer) (HarperCollins, June 1993)
*The Delectable Apple* by Kathleen Desmond Stang, Lynne Riding (Illustrator) (Chronicle Books, October 1994)
www.appleprocessors.org
www.urbanext.uiuc.edu/apples/varieties.html
www.easypickinsorchard.com
www.foodsubs.com/Apples.html
www.greatbritishkitchen.co.uk
www.usapple.org
www.cas.psu.edu/demos/fruit/

## BEER

*Beer Companion: A Connoisseur's Guide to the World's Finest Craft Beers* by Stephen Snyder (Simon & Schuster, November 1996)
*The Beer Lover's Rating Guide: Revised Edition* by Bob Klein (Workman Publishing Company, October 2000)
*The Encyclopedia of Beer: The Beer Lover's Bible—A Complete Reference to Beer Styles, Brewing Methods, Ingredients, Festivals, Traditions, and More* by Christine P. Rhodes (Henry Holt & Company, December 1995)
*Michael Jackson's Beer Companion: The World's Great Beer Styles, Gastronomy, and Traditions* by Michael Jackson (Running Press, September 1993)
*A Taste for Beer* by Stephen Beaumont (Storey Books, October 1995)
*Ultimate Beer* by Michael Jackson (DK Publishing, September 1998)
www.brewersassociation.org
www.beerinstitute.org
www.beermonthclub.com
www.evansale.com

## GENERAL

*Zingerman's Guide to Good Eating: How to Choose the Best Bread, Cheeses, Olive Oil, Pasta, Chocolate, and Much More* by Ari Weinzweig
September 2005 *Wine Spectator*
www.answers.com
www.foodreference.com
www.wikipedia.com

## • ACKNOWLEDGMENTS •

I couldn't have landed this incredible project without the help of food writer Andrew Friedman, and my fabulous agent, Joy Tutela. Thanks as well to my talented editor, Anja Schmidt. My gratitude also extends to the crew responsible for this book's gorgeous pages: gifted designer, Jee Chang, and art directors Michelle Baxter and Dirk Kaufman, as well as photographer Charles Schiller, prop stylist Betty Blau, and food stylists Tracy Harlor and Patricia White.

My appreciation goes out to those who fact-checked the chapters: Patricia Darragh at California Olive Oil Council, Ryan MacDonnell at Round Pond Olive Oil, Joe Simrany at Tea Association of the USA, The American Cheese Society, Paula Lambert at Mozzarella Company, Mike and John Harney at Harney & Sons Teas, Leah Porter at Chocolate Manufacturers Association, Jami Yanoski at National Honey Board, US Apple Association, Dr. Robert M. Crassweller at PSU College of Agricultural Sciences, Armandino Batali at Salumi Cured Meats, Gianluca Guglielmi at AG Ferrari, Kim Sayid at Barilla, Ray Daniels and Brewer's Association, Alex Milligan at Sherry-Lehmann, and Leslie Stein at Monell Chemical Senses Center.

Thanks to Harriet, David, and Jackie Cheney (who tested most of the recipes); Thelma and Herbert Cherry; Shira Boss-Bicak; Cassie Bowman (who inspired me to write this book); Christine Boyd; Lynn Cannici; Abby Cline; Rebecca Freedman; and Leticia Schwartz. They spent hours discussing this project with me or attended several tasting parties. Finally, thanks, above all, to my husband, Koby, for his endless love, support, and editing! I couldn't ask for a better partner or best friend.

## • CREDITS •

### PROP CREDITS
ALESSI
from www.fitzsu.com
Pp. 38–39  corkscrew

BODUM
T: 1 800 23BODUM
www.bodumusa.com
Pp. 156–159  Double Wall Sake Glass
Pp. 248–249 Corona Juice Glasses

LEKKER HOME
T: 1 888 753 5537
www.lekkerhome.com
Pp. 40–41 Blomus Stainless Tray
Pp. 98–99 Sage Coupe Bowl
Pp. 112–113 Porcelain Spoons
Pp. 180–181 Cocoon Tray Small
Pp. 246–247 Basis Glass Pitcher Small

RIEDEL, The Wine Glass Company
T: 1-888-4RIEDEL
www.riedel.com
Pp. 16–17 Dominus Wine Decanter
Pp. 40–41 Overture Series Wine Glass
Pp. 66–67 "O" Series Wine Glass
Pp. 180–181 "O" Series Wine Glasses
Pp. 222–223 "O" Series wine Glasses
Pp. 222–227 "Longdrink" beer glass

SEASONS INTERNATIONAL
T: 212 226 0797
www.seasonsintl.com
Pp. 118–119 reversible linen coasters
Pp. 134–135 Tea Ceremony set

TAKASHIMAYA, NY
T: 1 800 753 2038
Pp. 98–99 Green Linen napkin
Pp. 116–117 Tea Cup
Pp. 138–139 Tea Cups
and Iron Tea Pot